Oracle DBA
Pocket Guide

Oracle DBA
Pocket Guide

David C. Kreines

O'REILLY®

Beijing · Cambridge · Farnham · Köln · Paris · Sebastopol · Taipei · Tokyo

Oracle DBA Pocket Guide
by David C. Kreines

Published by O'Reilly Media, Inc., 1005 Gravenstein Highway North, Sebastopol, CA 95472.

O'Reilly books may be purchased for educational, business, or sales promotional use. Online editions are also available for most titles (*safari.oreilly.com*). For more information, contact our corporate/institutional sales department: (800) 998-9938 or *corporate@oreilly.com*.

Editor:	Deborah Russell
Production Editor:	Claire Cloutier
Cover Designer:	Ellie Volckhausen
Interior Designer:	David Futato

Printing History:

August 2005:   First Edition.

0-596-10049-3
[C]

Contents

Oracle DBA Pocket Guide

Introduction

The Oracle database has been a dominant force in the database market for more than two decades. Oracle Corporation has achieved this enviable position by providing a product that is compatible, scalable, portable, and capable of performing incredibly fast. The advantages Oracle holds over its competition come with a price, however—the Oracle database is a very complex product, and is becoming more so with every release. As a result, database administration has become critical, and the database administrator (DBA) has become key to the successful implementation of Oracle.

This book is a quick reference whose goal is to help Oracle DBAs, as well as designers and developers, make more effective use of their time and resources. It is designed to present useful information about administering the Oracle database in a clear, concise, and easy-to-use form.

This book focuses on the most recent Oracle releases, Oracle Database 10*g* and Oracle9*i* Database, with occasional references to earlier versions as needed.

Acknowledgments

Thanks to all those who helped in the conception and production of this book. I am especially grateful to Arup Nanda, an experienced DBA and author, who did a thorough and very timely technical review on the text. Many thanks to the staff at O'Reilly Media for handling the production of this book, and especially to my editor, Debby Russell.

Conventions

The following typographical conventions are used in this book:

UPPERCASE
> Indicates an Oracle keyword.

Italic
> Indicates filenames, directory names, URLs, and arguments or options to be replaced with user-supplied values; also used for emphasis or the introduction of a new technical term.

Bold
> Indicates the default within a list of options for a command or a parameter.

`Constant width`
> Used for code examples and for syntax models in command reference sections.

`Constant width italic`
> Used in code examples and command reference sections to indicate values that the user supplies.

[ ]
> Used in syntax models to enclose optional items.

{ }
> Used in syntax models to enclose a set of items from which you must choose exactly one.

|
> Used in syntax models to separate the items enclosed in curly brackets, such as {TRUE | FALSE}.

Oracle Architecture

This section provides a brief overview of the architecture of Oracle Database 10*g* and Oracle9*i* Database.

Database Versus Instance

For most Oracle users, the terms *database* and *instance* are used synonymously. However, there are differences that become especially important if you are running in Oracle's parallel environment: Real Application Clusters (or RAC, formerly known as Oracle Parallel Server, or OPS). Simply put, the *database* is the data on disk, stored in operating system files (or possibly, under Unix, in raw files), while the *instance* is composed of system memory and the background processes. The instance is STARTed using Oracle Enterprise Manager (OEM) or SQL*Plus. The database is then MOUNTed by the instance and is finally OPENed. The users CONNECT to the instance in order to access the data in the database. Figure 1 shows the basic components of the Oracle database and instance.

Except in a parallel environment, there is a one-to-one correspondence between instance and database. In the parallel world, the database can be MOUNTed by multiple instances.

Background Processes

The background processes reside in memory, are executed by the processor(s), and are responsible for the proper operation of the database. Depending on the options configured, there may be from 6 to 35 (or even more) background processes. Each background process has a specific responsibility and task to perform.

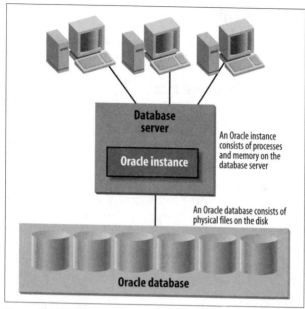

Figure 1. Oracle database and instance

The major Oracle background processes are:

SMON

> The System Monitor is responsible for monitoring the system and performing actions on it as required, such as coalescing free space in the database and managing recovery in case of an instance failure.

PMON

> The Process Monitor is responsible for detecting dropped user connections and responding with the appropriate actions, including managing locks, rolling back transactions, and removing the user process from the active process list. PMON also provides information about the instance to the Listener process when a new connection is requested.

DBW*n*

The Database Writer is responsible for writing data blocks from the buffer cache to the datafiles on disk. Up to 20 DBW*n* processes can be established (this is controlled by the DB_WRITER_PROCESS initialization parameter), and they are named DBW0 through DBW9, and then DBWA through DBWJ.

LGWR

The Log Writer is responsible for writing redo information to the redo log files on disk.

CKPT

The Checkpoint process is responsible for recording the System Change Number (SCN) in the header of each datafile and in each control file each time a checkpoint occurs (at least at every log file switch).

ARC*n*

The Archiver process is present whenever the database is running in archivelog mode, and is responsible for copying log files to one or more locations specified by the LOG_ARCHIVE_DEST initialization parameter whenever the log file is filled. There may be up to 10 ARC*n* processes, named ARC0 through ARC9; the number is controlled by the LOG_ARCHIVE_MAX_PROCESSES parameter.

RECO

The Recoverer process is responsible for recovering failed distributed transactions—that is, transactions involving tables on two or more different databases.

The operation of these background processes is controlled by the values specified in the Oracle initialization file, usually known as the *INIT.ORA* file or *SPFILE*. See the later section "Initialization Parameters" for additional information.

System Global Area

The System Global Area (SGA) is the shared memory area used by the instance to store information that must be shared between the database and the user processes. The SGA is composed of at least three main areas: the database buffer cache, the shared pool, and the redo log buffer. Optionally, it may also contain the large pool and the Streams pool, if defined. Figure 2 shows the SGA and its interaction with other Oracle components.

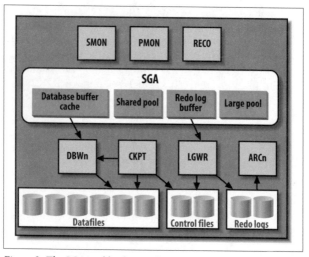

Figure 2. The SGA and background processes

Database buffer cache

The database buffer cache stores blocks of data retrieved from the database. This buffer between the users' requests and the actual datafiles improves the performance of the Oracle database. If a piece of data can be found in the buffer cache, it can be retrieved from memory; this uses less overhead than reading from disk. Oracle removes objects from the cache according to a least-recently-used (LRU) algorithm; thus, when a user requests data that was recently used, the data is more likely to be in the cache and Oracle can deliver it immediately, without having to execute a disk read operation.

Three buffer pools may be used by the cache:

DEFAULT
> The standard Oracle database buffer pool. All objects are cached here unless otherwise indicated.

KEEP
> For frequently used objects you want to cache.

RECYCLE
> For objects that you're less likely to access again.

The LRU algorithm does not operate on objects in the KEEP and RECYCLE buffer pools.

You can mark a table or index for caching in a specific buffer pool. This helps to keep more desirable objects in the cache and avoids the "churn" of all objects fighting for space in one central cache.

Shared pool

The shared pool caches various constructs that can be shared among users. For example, SQL statements issued by users are cached so that they can be reused if the same statement is submitted again. Another example is stored procedures— pieces of code stored and executed within the database. These are loaded into the shared pool for execution and then cached, again using an LRU algorithm. The shared pool is also used for caching information from the Oracle *data dictionary*, which is the metadata that describes the structure and content of the database itself.

Redo log buffer

The redo log buffer caches redo information in order to improve performance. Oracle caches the information until it can be written to the redo log on disk at a more optimal time, which avoids the overhead of constantly writing to disk.

Large pool

The large pool is an optional area of the SGA used for buffering I/O for various server processes, including those used for backup and recovery. The area is also used to store session memory for the Shared Server (formerly known as the Multi-Threaded Server, or MTS) and when using the XA protocol for distributed transactions.

Files

Four types of files are used by the Oracle instance: control files, datafiles, redo log files, and parameter files. When you START the instance, the parameter file is read. When you MOUNT the database, the control files are read. When you OPEN the database, the datafiles and redo log files are referenced. When a database is being updated, changes are recorded in the online redo log files, which provide a mechanism for recovery in case of a failure.

Parameter files

These files (either the *INIT.ORA* file or the *SPFILE*) specify how the instance is configured and point to the control files. These files are not part of the instance, but must exist to start the instance.

Control file

The control file contains a list of all the other files that make up the database. It also contains key information about the contents and state of the database, such as:

- The name of the database
- The date when the database was created
- The current state of the datafiles: whether they need recovery, are in a read-only state, and so on
- Whether the database closed cleanly the last time it was shut down
- The time period covered by each archived redo log
- The backups that have been performed for the database

The control file can easily grow in size to 10 MB or more. The size is influenced by a number of initialization parameters and parameters specified during the database creation, including MAXLOGFILES, MAXLOGMEMBERS, MAX_LOG_HISTORY, MAXDATAFILES, and MAXINSTANCES.

You can (and should) have your Oracle instance maintain multiple copies of control files. Although you can potentially rebuild a control file if it is damaged or deleted, this process requires that the database be shut down; in some scenarios, you will not be able to rebuild the control file to its correct state. You cannot run an Oracle database without a control file, so having multiple copies of your control file can be an important safety measure. You use the initialization parameter CONTROL_FILES to list the locations of multiple copies of the control file.

Datafiles

Datafiles contain the actual data stored in the database, including the tables and indexes created by users of the database; the data dictionary (which keeps information about these data structures); and the rollback or redo segments (which are used to implement Oracle's consistency scheme).

A datafile is composed of Oracle database blocks that are, in turn, composed of operating system blocks on a disk. Oracle block sizes range from 2 KB to 32 KB. If you're using Oracle with very large memory (VLM) support, you may use big Oracle blocks (BOBs), which can be as large as 64 KB in size.

You set a default block size for the database, but you can also have five different nonstandard block sizes in the database. Each datafile can support only one block size, but you can have mixed block sizes within the database.

Datafiles belong to only one database and to only one tablespace within that database. Data is read in units of Oracle blocks from the datafiles into memory as required. Blocks of data are written from memory to the datafiles when blocks are changed.

Datafiles are the lowest level of granularity between an Oracle database and the operating system. When you plan a database on the I/O subsystem, the smallest physical piece you place in any particular location is a datafile. Tuning the I/O subsystem to improve Oracle performance often involves moving datafiles from one set of disks to another.

Datafile structure. The first block of each datafile, called the *datafile header*, contains critical information used to maintain the overall integrity of the database. One of the most crucial pieces of information in this header is the *checkpoint structure*, a logical timestamp that indicates the last point at which changes were written to the datafile. This timestamp is critical for recovery situations. The Oracle recovery process uses the timestamp in the header of a datafile to determine which redo logs to apply to bring the datafile up to the current point in time.

Extents and segments. From a physical point of view, a datafile is stored as operating system blocks. From a logical point of view, datafiles have three intermediate organizational levels: data blocks, extents, and segments. An *extent* is a set of data blocks that are contiguous within an Oracle datafile. A *segment* is an object (such as a table or an index) that is stored as one or more extents.

When Oracle updates data that makes the row longer, it attempts to use the same data block for the additional space. If there is not enough room in the data block for the new information, Oracle will write the additional data to a new data block, which may be in a different extent. This is known as *block chaining*, and it should be avoided because it results in more disk I/O when accessing the data.

Redo log files

Redo log files store the changes made to the database. In normal operation, Oracle caches changed blocks in memory. In the event of an instance failure, some of the changed blocks may not have been written out to the datafiles, and the redo log can be used to "play back" the changes that were lost when the failure occurred.

Multiplexing redo log files. Oracle uses specific terminology in describing the management of redo logs. Each Oracle instance records the changes it makes to the database in redo logs. You can have one or more redo logs, referred to as *redo log members*, in a *redo log group*.

Logically, you can think of a redo log group as a single redo log file. However, Oracle allows you to specify multiple copies of a redo log to protect the log against media failure. Multiple copies of the same log are grouped together in a redo log group. All redo log groups for an instance are referred to as a *redo thread*.

WARNING

There is no way to reproduce a lost redo log file, so be sure that you have multiple copies of the redo file.

Log file use. Once Oracle fills one redo log file, it automatically begins to use the next log file. Once the server cycles through all the available redo log files, it returns to the first one and reuses it. Oracle keeps track of the different redo logs by using a sequence number. As the server fills each redo log file and moves on to the next one, it increments an internal counter called the *redo log sequence number*. This sequence number is recorded inside the redo log files as they are used. Oracle uses this internal number to properly sequence the logs, even though a reused log file may have the name initially created for an earlier redo log.

Archived redo logs. It is possible to lose critical information in the redo log when Oracle cycles over a previously used redo log. In order to avoid this problem, it is advisable to archive the redo logs as they fill.

There are actually two types of redo logs for Oracle:

Online redo logs
> The operating system files that Oracle cycles through to log the changes made to the database

Archived redo logs
> Copies of the filled online redo logs made to avoid losing redo data as the online redo logs are overwritten

An Oracle database can run in one of two modes with respect to archiving redo logs:

NOARCHIVELOG
> As the name implies, no redo logs are archived. As Oracle cycles through the logs, the filled logs are reinitialized and overwritten, which erases the history of the changes made to the database. Choosing not to archive redo logs significantly reduces your choices and options for database backups.

ARCHIVELOG

When Oracle rolls over to a new redo log, it archives the previous redo log. To prevent gaps in the history, a given redo log cannot be reused until it has been successfully archived. The archived redo logs, with the online redo logs, provide a complete history of all changes made to the database and allow Oracle to recover all committed transactions up to the exact time a failure occurred.

To enable archivelog mode, do the following:

- Turn on archive logging with the ALTER DATABASE ARCHIVELOG command in SQL*Plus.
- Set the LOG_ARCHIVE_START initialization parameter to TRUE. This will start archiving logs to the location specified by the LOG_ARCHIVE_DEST parameters with the names specified by the LOG_ARCHIVE_FORMAT parameter.

Logical Database Structures

In addition to the physical files used by the database, Oracle maintains many types of logical structures. Some of the most important are summarized here:

Tablespaces

The basic storage allocation in an Oracle database is a tablespace. Each tablespace is composed of one or more physical (operating system) files. Every database is created with the SYSTEM tablespace. Other tablespaces are created by the DBA. Note, however, that if you allow the Oracle Installer to create a database automatically, it will create additional tablespaces.

Schemas

In Oracle, a schema is essentially the same as an account or a username. Each object in the database is owned by a schema. Every Oracle database is created with two initial schemas: SYS, which is used to store the data dictionary, and SYSTEM, which often stores some data dictionary extensions, as well as critical tables for other tools. Other schemas are created by the DBA. Each schema can be granted quotas in any tablespace. There is no necessary relationship between a schema and a tablespace.

Segments

Each object that takes up space is created as one or more segments. Each segment can be in one, and only one, tablespace.

Extents

Each segment is composed of one or more extents. An extent is a contiguous allocation of space within a data-file of a tablespace. At the time a segment is created, you can specify the size of the initial and next extents, as well as the minimum and maximum number of extents.

Rollback or undo segments

Every time you update a table, Oracle writes the old value into either an undo segment or a rollback segment. This allows other users to maintain a consistent read on the table. It also allows Oracle to restore the contents of the table in the event that you do not commit the change.

Temporary segments

Temporary segments are used by Oracle during table and index creation and for sorting, as well as for temporary storage required for other operations, such as hash joins.

Tables

All data in a database is stored in tables. Data includes not only user data, but also the contents of the data dictionary.

Indexes

Indexes are used both to facilitate the quick retrieval of data from the table and to enforce the uniqueness of column values. Indexes are stored in separate segments from the table data, except for index-organized tables, which are actually indexes that contain all the data.

Software Options

The Oracle relational database management system (RDBMS) is sold as a base product with options. Typically, new functionality is first introduced as an extra-cost option and is then bundled into the base product in later releases. The information provided here is current at the time of publication. Please contact your Oracle sales representative or the Oracle web site (*http://www.oracle.com*) for additional information.

Base Product

There are several different editions of the Oracle database:

Standard Edition
> The basic server edition of Oracle, which does not include all the capabilities of the Oracle database. There are extra options described below that cannot be used with the Standard Edition.

Enterprise Edition
> The complete Oracle database, which is required for the use of the extra options described below.

Personal Edition
> A single-user version of the Oracle database, available only for Windows. This edition includes all the functionality of most of the options in the Enterprise Edition, where appropriate.

Lite
> A trimmed-down version of the Oracle database designed for mobile use.

In addition, there is a version called Standard Edition One, which is identical to the Standard Edition except that it is licensed for a maximum of two processors.

The following options are available for the Enterprise Edition (and are not available with the Standard Edition):

Partitioning
OLAP
Data Mining
Spatial
Advanced Security
Label Security
Configuration Management Pack
Tuning Pack
Diagnostics Pack

Licensing

Oracle products are currently licensed using two different licensing models:

Per Named User

This option licenses the product to a specified number of specific individual users. Under this model, you must include all users of the database, regardless of whether they use the database concurrently. For example, if 20 users make use of the database, you must be licensed for 20 named users, even if only 5 of them are ever connected at the same time.

Per Processor

This model licenses the product to the server, rather than individual users, and allows an unlimited number of users to be connected to the database. Each processor on the server must be licensed, and so a server with four processors must have a four-processor license.

These two basic licensing models are offered with various terms:

Perpetual
> The license is good forever. Note, however, that you cannot upgrade to newer versions unless Oracle Support is also purchased.

Two Year
> The license is good for two years, and then ends. At that point, you must purchase a new license or stop using the product.

Four Year
> The license is good for four years, and then ends. At that point, you must purchase a new license or stop using the product.

Version Numbers

Oracle version numbers may appear confusing when you first encounter them. The RDBMS uses a four-digit version number—for example, 9.2.4.2. In this number:

- The first digit refers to a *major release* of the RDBMS.
- The second digit refers to a *minor release* of the RDBMS. The first two digits together define a *release level* whose functionality has been defined and documented by Oracle Corporation.
- The third digit refers to a *code release* by the base engineering group for the release level.
- The fourth digit defines a *patch set* of specific cumulative patches to the code release.

The version number referenced above, 9.2.4.2, is the second patch set to the fourth code release of the 9.2 functionality.

NOTE

Some Oracle releases (most notably those for Unix platforms) use a five-digit numbering system, but the fifth digit is almost always 0 or 1.

Configuration Planning

Once your organization has decided which Oracle options to acquire, you need to start planning the implementation. Here are some of the areas you will have to consider.

Availability

One of the most important functions of the DBA is to provide for the continued availability of the information in the database. Before implementing the database, you need to decide how long you can afford to be down in the event of an emergency, as well as how long you can be down for normal maintenance. How you answer these questions determines what kind of redundancy you need to build into your configuration and dictates how you will perform backups and standard system maintenance.

A number of Oracle facilities can help guarantee availability; you should consider the use of replication, a hot standby database, and Real Application Clusters (RAC), described briefly in the following sections.

Replication

Replication allows you to maintain separate databases, where the updates that are performed to one database are automatically propagated to the others. These redundant databases can be used both to maintain local copies of data (eliminating long network propagation delays) and to provide a second copy of the data (which can continue to be used if one of the databases fails). Once the failed database is brought back online, all updates that have occurred since the failure will be automatically applied to the database.

Replication does require that you completely duplicate the entire physical implementation, including multiple computer systems and storage. You will also have to implement a reasonably fast network communication link between the multiple computer systems. However, replication can be used to survive not only hardware or software problems, but also sitewide emergencies (assuming, of course, that the replicated database is running offsite).

Hot standby database

With a hot standby database, you actually use only one database at a time. The second database is constantly in recovery mode. As an archived redo log file is generated, it is copied over to the remote site and applied to the database. In the event of a failure of the primary database, you complete the recovery process and bring up the standby database.

With this facility, you will have to maintain redundant computer and storage systems, and in the event of a recovery, you may have lost any committed transactions that have not yet been moved to an archived log file. However, you will not need to maintain a high-speed communication line between the databases, as you must with replication. In fact, the connection does not even have to be continuous.

Real Application Clusters (RAC)

Real Application Clusters (RAC) allow multiple computer systems to share a common database. With RAC, you will be able to survive the failure of a single computer system as long as your shared disk storage remains available. You will still need to maintain redundant computer systems, and you should use a redundant disk technology. However, the additional computer systems can be used simultaneously, thereby providing a powerful tool for load balancing.

Backup and Recovery

Even with modern redundant hardware, you will still need to back up your database. You can do this through a logical backup (export) or a physical backup at the datafile level. As you'd expect, there are tradeoffs with each mechanism in terms of how long it takes to recover, how long the database might be unavailable, and how consistent the backup is. For more details on the available backup and recovery methods, see "Backup and Recovery," later in this book.

Performance

Performance is a somewhat nebulous term; everyone has a different idea about what it means. Performance can be measured by how fast one person can get a long query done; by how many people can perform concurrent online transaction processing (OLTP) transactions; or by how fast a given batch job runs. Good performance for one user may mean poor performance for another, so it is important to define your expectations before pursuing performance improvements. Performance can, however, be measured objectively; therefore, changes to the system can be observed and quantified.

Performance is impacted by how queries are written, how disks are laid out, the amount of memory, and the speed of the CPU, disk, and bus. You will probably need to work with your system administrator and/or hardware vendor to determine whether your system has sufficient capacity to provide good performance.

Memory

The more memory you can acquire for your computer system, the better. In fact, adding memory is typically the best way to improve performance. In addition to Oracle's using memory for the SGA, the operating system will use memory to track each process and handle disk I/O. You want sufficient memory to allow the entire SGA to remain in memory, in order to avoid swapping and paging. Of course, adding memory is only the first step; Oracle must be configured to utilize the additional memory—for example, by adding more database buffers or shared pool space.

Disk layout

Oracle, like all relational databases, will probably be I/O bound. The second most important way to improve performance (after adding more memory) is to improve the overall performance of the I/O system. The more disks you can provide to Oracle, the better your I/O performance will be. Remember that for each table update you perform, Oracle will perform the following disk I/Os:

- The write to the table
- Updates to any indexes
- Rollback information for the table and indexes
- Redo log buffer writes to disk for the table and indexes
- Updates to the data dictionary if new extents are needed

For the best performance, follow these guidelines when you are laying out the disk subsystem:

- Allocate separate disks for data, redo logs, and archive files.
- Use multiple controllers when available.
- Use disk striping (either by the operating system or by Oracle).
- Keep data and index segments on separate disks for a given table.
- Use a separate disk for the undo tablespace or rollback segments.
- Keep the system tablespace on a separate disk or a lightly used disk.
- Avoid the use of RAID-5 disks (RAID stands for redundant arrays of inexpensive disks) for high-write files. Such files include undo or rollback segments, temporary tablespaces, redo logs, and tables with high amounts of inserts, updates, and deletes. RAID-5 maintains data and parity information on multiple disks. The time spent reading, calculating, and writing to multiple disks will impact your total performance.

Installation

This section summarizes the basics of the Oracle installation process. Consult the *Installation Guide* for your system for specific information.

Planning

While it is possible to simply insert the Oracle CD and start installing, experienced DBAs know that this technique will almost certainly require additional work and probably a re-installation in the near future. It is far better to spend some time up front planning the Oracle installation. Some of the more important decisions to be made are:

- Decide the name of the database (specified in the DB_NAME initialization parameter) and the domain that the database will belong to (specified in the DB_DOMAIN parameter).

- Determine the initial size of the database, taking into account the system and temporary tablespaces, as well as data and index storage requirements.

- Decide on the initial tablespace names.

- Decide whether to use Automatic Undo Management and, if it is used, the name and size of the undo tablespace.

- Carefully plan the physical locations of database datafiles, keeping in mind the performance guidelines discussed above.

- Decide on the locations for control files. Where possible, try to locate control files on at least two different disk controllers.

- Plan the initial set of initialization parameters and decide whether you will use an *INIT.ORA* file or an *SPFILE*.

- Determine your initial default block size (specified in the DB_BLOCK_SIZE parameter). Remember that although Oracle supports multiple block sizes, the default block size cannot be changed after database creation.
- Plan for the initial set of users, including the method for authenticating users and the roles and privileges to be assigned to each.

Installing the Oracle Software

The Oracle software is installed using the Oracle Universal Installer (OUI), which is provided on the installation CD for all Oracle platforms. The OUI is a Java tool that provides essentially the same user interface regardless of your platform. Note that under Unix and Linux, the OUI requires an X Windows environment; under Microsoft Windows, the OUI runs in native Windows mode.

The actual operation of the OUI is straightforward and intuitive. Depending on your installation CD set, you may be asked to choose the edition (Enterprise, Standard, etc.) you want to install. The OUI will then suggest a list of database options and components, which you can modify. Once you have told the program what you want to install, the installation proceeds automatically.

You have the option to create a "starter" database. If you choose this option, the Database Creation Assistant (DBCA) will be invoked and you will be prompted for some basic configuration information.

Creating a Database

There are two ways to create a database: using the DBCA or manually.

Using the DBCA

The DBCA can be invoked during installation or by using the *dbca* command at any later time. The DBCA is a graphical tool that can be used to:

- Create a database
- Configure options in a database
- Delete a database
- Add a customized database creation template for use with the DBCA

The DBCA has three preconfigured database creation templates available "out of the box:" Data Warehouse, General-Purpose, and Transaction Processing. If you are not sure how the database will be used, choose General-Purpose.

As you proceed through the program screens, you will be given the opportunity to provide information about the database to be created, including:

- Database Identification
- Management Options
- Database Credentials
- Storage Options
- Database File Locations
- Recovery Configuration
- Database Content (simple schemas)
- Initialization Parameters
- Database Storage

Once you have provided all the information required by the DBCA, you will be given the option to create the database and/or save your work as a database template. You will then be shown a summary of the creation template. If you chose to create the database, then when you click OK the database will be created and the instance will be started.

Creating a database manually

Many DBAs prefer to create the database manually using SQL*Plus. Follow these steps:

1. Create an *INIT.ORA* file containing the basic initialization parameters for the database. This file should be located in the default directory: *$ORACLE_HOME/dbs* in Unix and Linux, or *$ORACLE_HOME\database* in Windows. Note that Oracle provides a sample *INIT.ORA* file when the software is installed.

2. Connect using SQL*Plus:

   ```
   sqlplus /nolog
   connect SYS as sysdba
   ```

3. Create an *SPFILE*:

   ```
   create spfile from pfile;
   ```

4. Start the instance:

   ```
   startup nomount
   ```

5. Run the CREATE DATABASE command—for example:

   ```
   CREATE DATABASE "DB1"
        maxinstances   2
        maxlogfiles    6
        maxlogmembers 5
        maxdatafiles 1000
        character set "US7ASCII"
        user SYS identified by darth_vader
        user SYSTEM identified by cheese$teak
   datafile '/disk00/oracle10/oradata/DB1/system01.dbf'
        size 300M
   extent management local
   sysaux datafile
             '/disk00/oracle10/oradata/DB1/sysaux01.dbf'
                 size 300M
   logfile  group 1 '/disk01/oracle10/oradata/DB1/log01.log'
                 size 512K,
             group 2 '/disk01/oracle/oradata/DB1/log02.log'
                 size 512K,
             group 3 '/disk01/oracle/oradata/DB1/log03.log'
                 size 512K
   default tablespace users
   ```

```
default temporary tablespace temp tempfile '/disk01/
oracle10/oradata/DB1/temp01.dbf' size 50M
undo tablespace undo datafile '/disk02/oracle10/
oradata/DB1/undo01.dbf' size 500M autoextend on;
```

6. Run scripts to create the data dictionary:

```
start catalog.sql
start catproc.sql
```

7. Create additional tablespaces.

8. Create additional users and assign each to a default tablespace.

9. Make a backup of your new database.

Initialization Parameters

Oracle is a very flexible and configurable system. These two qualities are absolutely necessary for a database that can be run on dozens of different hardware platforms in a multitude of configurations, supporting an almost infinite variety of applications and users. In order to achieve the needed flexibility, Oracle provides a simple method of specifying certain operational characteristics of the database in a clear and consistent manner. DBAs specify most of these characteristics by setting and resetting values for the database *initialization parameters*, commonly referred to as *INIT.ORA parameters*. The goal is to set these parameters in a way that maximizes database performance while minimizing DBA maintenance and resulting downtime.

The following is a typical initialization file for a general-purpose installation of Oracle:

```
DB_NAME = "ORAC"
DB_DOMAIN = oraserver
INSTANCE_NAME = ORAC
SERVICE_NAMES = ORAC.oraserver

DB_FILES = 1024
DB_BLOCK_SIZE = 8192
```

```
COMPATIBLE = 9.2.0
SORT_AREA_SIZE = 65536
SORT_AREA_RETAINED_SIZE = 65536

CONTROL_FILES =
(disk0/oracle/oradata/ORAC/control01.ctl,
 disk1/oracle/oradata/ORAC/control02.ctl,
 disk2/oracle/oradata/ORAC/control03.ctl)

OPEN_CURSORS = 100
CURSOR_SHARING = similar

MAX_ENABLED_ROLES = 30
DB_FILE_MULTIBLOCK_READ_COUNT = 8
DB_CACHE_SIZE = 2048

SHARED_POOL_SIZE = 19728640
LARGE_POOL_SIZE = 614400
JAVA_POOL_SIZE = 25971520

LOG_CHECKPOINT_INTERVAL = 10000
LOG_CHECKPOINT_TIMEOUT = 1800
```

Note that each parameter typically begins on a new line, and complex parameters may span multiple lines. Whitespace may be used for readability.

The name and location of the database initialization parameter file on your system depends upon the Oracle version and the operating system you are running, as described in the following sections.

INIT.ORA: The Initialization File

In Oracle releases prior to Oracle9i Database Release 1, initialization parameters were always specified in a file referred to as the *INIT.ORA* file. Starting with that release, initialization parameters could be (and most often are) stored in the *SPFILE* (see the next section). However, even if you're running more recent releases, you always have the option of using the *INIT.ORA* file, and so I describe it here. The actual filename is usually in the form init<*SID*>.ora, where <*SID*> is the SID, or system identifier, for your particular Oracle instance. The SID is a unique name that is used to identify a particular instance across your entire environment. Typically, the *INIT.ORA* file is located in the *$ORACLE_HOME/dbs* directory.

NOTE

Refer to the Oracle documentation for the default location of this file for your particular operating system.

You must be sure to store the *INIT.ORA* file in a location where it is accessible to the client that's starting the database.

Because the *INIT.ORA* file is a simple text file, it can be modified using any ASCII editor. However, be careful not to use a word-processing program like Microsoft Word to edit the *INIT.ORA* file; doing so can easily make the file unreadable by Oracle. If you must use Word to create or modify the file, be sure to save it as a plain ASCII text file.

Parameters are typically entered into the file with one parameter and value per line, as shown in the previous example. Comments may be added after a parameter or on their own line (preceded by the # symbol):

```
# The following line contains a comment
DB_FILE_MULTIBLOCK_READ_COUNT = 8    # Do not change
```

SPFILE: The Server Parameter File

The server parameter file, known as the *SPFILE*, differs from the standard *INIT.ORA* file in a number of ways:

- It is a binary file, rather than a text-based file.
- It is stored on the server, rather than on a client machine.
- It can maintain changes to parameter values over the shutdown and startup of an instance.

This last property is what distinguishes *SPFILE*. Any changes you make to configuration parameters via the ALTER SYSTEM command will be saved as part of the permanent configuration file. As a result, you can change any of your database parameter values for tuning purposes without having to manually update an *INIT.ORA* file in order to retain the new values.

You also have the option of making dynamic changes to parameters without making them a part of the *SPFILE*; you do this by including the SCOPE clause in the ALTER SYSTEM command, using the following syntax:

```
ALTER SYSTEM SET parameter_name = parameter_value
    SCOPE = {MEMORY | SPFILE | BOTH};
```

Even if you are running with an *SPFILE*, you can still use a local *INIT.ORA* file by specifying the location of that file with a PFILE=*name* clause in the STARTUP command. For example:

```
STARTUP PFILE=/home/oracle/myinit.ora
```

Releases from Oracle9*i* Database onward also provide a simple way to migrate the parameters in an existing *INIT.ORA* file to the binary *SPFILE* for an instance. You can copy the *INIT.ORA* file to the server machine (if it's not already there) and issue the following command from SQL*Plus, substituting the complete actual pathname for *pathname*:

```
CREATE SPFILE FROM PFILE='pathname/initsid.ora';
```

By default, the *SPFILE* is located in the *$ORACLE_HOME/dbs* directory. The SPFILE parameter, which you can specify in your *INIT.ORA* file, allows you to point to a nondefault location for the *SPFILE* by including a line such as the following in your file:

```
SPFILE=$ORACLE_HOME/dbs/spfile.ora;
```

Dynamic and Static Parameters

While most initialization parameters are static, taking their values from the initialization file as it exists at the time of database startup, some may be dynamically modified while the instance is up and the database is open.

Dynamic modification is different from dynamic storage of a changed value in the *SPFILE*. In all versions of Oracle, you can dynamically modify a setting using the ALTER SYSTEM or ALTER SESSION command. These changes may also be dynamically stored in the *SPFILE*, depending on the value of the SCOPE clause of the ALTER command.

Backup and Recovery

Even with redundant hardware, you will still need to back up your database. You can do this through a logical backup (export) or a physical backup at the datafile level. As you'd expect, there are trade-offs with each mechanism in terms of complexity, time to recover, how long the database might be unavailable, and how consistent the backup is.

There are four different methods available for backing up the Oracle database:

- The Export (EXP) and Import (IMP) utilities
- Data Pump Export and Import (beginning with Oracle Database 10g Release 1)
- User-managed backup and recovery
- Oracle-managed backup and recovery using Recovery Manager (RMAN)

Table 1 provides an overview of these methods; the following sections describe them in more detail.

Table 1. Comparison of Oracle's backup/recovery methods

Backup/recovery characteristic	EXP/IMP and Data Pump	User-managed	RMAN
Consistent/ inconsistent	Consistent, but only with database activity stopped or suspended for the table	Either	Either
Logical/physical	Logical	Physical	Physical
Full/incremental	Full	Full	Either; can back up only changed data blocks
Whole database/ tablespace	Tables only	Either	Either
Complete/incomplete recovery	Complete only	Either	Either
Datafile/block media recovery	Table-based recovery	Datafile only	Either

Export (EXP) and Import (IMP)

The Export utility, known as EXP, takes a logical backup of the database. EXP writes, in a proprietary format, all the SQL commands necessary both to recreate the database objects and to insert all the data. The companion Import utility, IMP, reads this file and executes all the statements.

NOTE

Starting with Oracle Database 10g Release 1, Oracle provides a pair of new utilities: Data Pump Export and Data Pump Import. From this release on, Oracle refers to EXP and IMP as Original Export and Original Import, respectively.

Import can be used to restore data created by the Export utility at a lower or equal version. For example, IMP Version 10.1 can restore data created by EXP Version 9.2, but cannot recover data created by EXP Version 10.2.

You can export at the database level, schema level, or table level, and you can import all of the export file or a portion of it. EXP and IMP are especially useful when you need to recover data that has been corrupted or lost as a result of human or application error. Export/Import (or, starting with Oracle Database 10g, Data Pump Export/Import) is the only backup method that allows you to recreate a single table. Be aware, however, that in a relational database, it may not be possible (or make sense) to recover only one table. Multiple tables may need to be recovered in order to maintain referential integrity.

NOTE

Recovery can be performed only to the state of the database at the time of the export. Any changes made to the database after the export will be lost.

In addition, Export is the only backup method that will allow you to recover your database to a different hardware platform running a different operating system—and perhaps even a different version of Oracle.

EXP and IMP commands

The EXP and IMP utilities can be run either interactively or via the command line.

NOTE

Before you run either EXP or IMP, you must create the appropriate data dictionary views by running the *catexp.sql* script (this script is run automatically as part of *catalog.sql*).

You can invoke these utilities interactively as follows:

```
EXP [username[[/password[{@service | AS SYSDBA]]
IMP [username[[/password[{@service | AS SYSDBA]]
```

The command-line format for EXP and IMP is:

```
exp [[/password[{@service | AS SYSDBA]] {parm=value ... |
    PARFILE=filename}
imp [[/password[{@service | AS SYSDBA]] {parm=value ... |
    PARFILE=filename}
```

username
> Username that will run the utility.

password
> Password for the specified username. If a password is not specified, the utilities will prompt for it.

service
> Oracle Net name that identifies the service.

parm = value
> Parameter name and value. There are three types of parameters: those that are common to EXP and IMP; those that are specific to EXP; and those that are specific to IMP. Multiple parameter/value pairs are separated from each other by spaces or commas. A single *value* for

a parameter can be in parentheses. Multiple *values* for a parameter must be in parentheses, separated by commas. The total length of the command cannot exceed the maximum length for a command on the platform-specific operating system.

PARFILE = *filename*

Specifies the name of a file that will contain parameters and values. Even if a parameter file is specified, you can also include parameters on the command line. If a parameter file and a command-line parameter both refer to the same parameter, the last mention on the command line takes precedence. For example, the value in the parameter file takes precedence if the PARFILE clause comes after the *parm=value* statement on the command line. Continuing with this example, if the PARFILE contains the parameter listing FULL=N, then EXP will not perform a full database export even if FULL=Y was specified on the command line.

Common Export/Import parameters

The following parameters can be used with both the Export and the Import utilities:

BUFFER = *buffersize*

Specifies the size, in bytes, of the buffer used to fetch or load rows. This parameter determines the maximum number of rows in an array fetched by the Export utility as:

> *buffersize / maximum_row_size*

If you specify 0, Export fetches one row at a time; Import loads one row at a time. Tables with LONG, LOB, BFILE, REF, ROWID, or type columns are always fetched or loaded one row at a time. BUFFER applies only to conventional path export and has no effect on a direct path export. The default is operating system dependent.

CONSTRAINTS = {**Y** | N}

Specifies whether table constraints are exported or imported.

FEEDBACK = *n*

When *n* is greater than 0, specifies that Export or Import should display a progress meter in the form of a dot for each *n* rows exported. The default is 0.

FILE = *filename*

Specifies the name of the file to be created by the export or used as the source of the import. This parameter can take multiple filenames for use with the FILESIZE parameter, as described in the next list item. The default extension is *.dmp*.

FILESIZE = *n*

Limits the size of an individual export file. If the export is larger than this specified size, Export will create multiple files, and multiple files can be specified in the FILES parameter to support this. The maximum number of bytes represented by *n* is limited by the operating system and version of Oracle. You must use the FILESIZE parameter when importing from an export file that was created using the FILESIZE parameter.

FULL = {Y | **N**}

When set to Y, Export performs a full database export, which exports all objects from the entire database; Import imports the entire export file. The EXP_FULL_DATABASE role is required to export in this mode.

GRANTS = {**Y** | N}

For the Export utility, specifies whether to export grants; for the Import utility, whether to import grants that were previously exported. The grants that are exported depend on whether you export in full database or user mode. In full database mode, all grants on a table are exported; in user mode, only those granted by the owner of the table are exported.

HELP = {Y | **N**}

Determines whether a help message with descriptions of the export and import parameters is displayed. (If HELP=Y, no export or import is performed.)

INDEXES = {**Y** | N}

For the Export utility, specifies whether to export all indexes; for Import, whether to create or update indexes after importing a table. INDEXES=N specifies that indexes are not to be exported. The use of INDEXES=Y for import assumes that the same parameter was used in the creation of the export file. System-generated indexes, such as Large Object (LOB) indexes, Oracle Internet Directory (OID) indexes, or unique constraint indexes, are recreated by Import regardless of the setting of this parameter.

LOG = *filename*

Specifies the name of an operating system file to receive informational and error messages. If this parameter is not used, messages will not be sent to a file. The default extension is *.log*.

RECORDLENGTH = *length*

Specifies the record length for the export file or the file to be imported. The value defaults to the standard for the host operating system. If you are transferring an export file for import on another system, you can use this parameter to match the default record length on the other system. You may also be able to improve the performance of a direct path export (DIRECT=Y) by increasing the RECORDLENGTH.

RESUMABLE = {Y | **N**}

Used to enable and disable resumable space allocation. This feature lets Oracle pause in the middle of an operation if the operation fails because it has run out of space.

RESUMABLE_NAME = *name*
> Used to identify the resumable operation for the operator. Requires RESUMABLE to be Y.

RESUMABLE_TIMEOUT = *n*
> Specifies the time, in seconds, that the operation will wait for the operator to resume it after allocating more space. The default is 7200.

ROWS = {**Y** | N}
> Specifies whether the rows of data in tables are included in the export or import. Specify ROWS=N to export the structure of all objects without their contents or to import the structures without any data.

TABLESPACES = (*tablespace_name*[, *tablespace_name* ...])
> For Export, exports all tables that exist in the listed tablespaces or that have a partition in a listed tablespace. For Import, specifies a list of the tablespaces to be imported.

USERID = *username/password@service*
> Specifies the *username/password@service* of the user initiating the export or import if it is not specified on the command line. *password* and *@service* (net service name) are optional; if you do not include them as part of the parameter, the utility will prompt you for them.

VOLSIZE = *n*
> Specifies the maximum number of bytes in an export file on a tape.

Export-only parameters

The following parameters can be used only with the Export utility:

COMPRESS = {**Y** | N}
> Specifies how Export manages the initial extent for table data. The default causes Export to write a CREATE command that will cause a subsequent import to create the object with all the exported data in a single initial extent.

If you specify COMPRESS=N, Export uses the current storage parameters, including the values of the INITIAL extent size and the NEXT extent size.

CONSISTENT = {Y | **N**}

Specifies whether Export uses the SET TRANSACTION READ ONLY statement to ensure both that the data seen by Export is consistent to a single point in time and that it does not change during the execution of the export. You should specify CONSISTENT=Y when you anticipate that other applications will update the database after an export has started.

DIRECT = {Y | **N**}

Specifies direct path or conventional path (the default) export. Direct path exports extract data by reading the data directly, bypassing the SQL processing layer; this can be much faster than a conventional path export. Direct path export cannot be used to export tables containing any of the following column types: REF, LOB, BFILE, or object type columns, which include VARRAYs and nested tables.

FLASHBACK_SCN = n

Indicates the System Change Number used for flashback on the export.

FLASHBACK_TIME = *time*

Indicates the time used for flashback on the export. Oracle identifies the SCN closest to this time and uses it for the export.

INCTYPE = {INCREMENTAL | CUMULATIVE}

INCREMENTAL exports all database objects that have changed since the last incremental, cumulative, or complete export, as tracked by the table SYS.INCEXP, then updates the table with a new ITIME and EXPID. CUMULATIVE exports all database objects that have changed since the last cumulative or complete export, as tracked by the table SYS.INCEXP, then updates the table with a new CTIME, ITIME, and EXPID. There is no default.

OBJECT_CONSISTENT = {Y | **N**}

Causes each object to be exported in its own transaction, as opposed to CONSISTENT, which uses a single transaction for the export. Introduced in Oracle9i Database Release 2.

OWNER = (*username*[, *username* ...])

If used, indicates that the export is a user-mode export and lists the user(s) whose objects will be exported.

QUERY = *query_clause*

The *query_clause* is a WHERE clause that is appended to the SELECT for each table or partition listed in the TABLE clause. The *query_clause* is a string, so it should be preceded and ended with a backslash and quotation mark (\"). If you need to use single quotes to delimit character strings in the query, use \'.

STATISTICS = {**ESTIMATE** | COMPUTE | NONE}

Specifies the type of SQL ANALYZE statements to generate when the exported data is restored using the Import utility.

TABLES = (*tablename*[, *tablename* ...])

Specifies that Export is to be run in table mode and lists the table and partition names to export. There is no default. The *tablename* may be specified as *schema.table*: *partition_name*, as follows:

schema

Specifies the name of the user's schema from which to export the table or partition. If omitted, the schema specified by USERID is used, except when FULL=Y is specified.

table

> Indicates the name of a table to be exported. If a table in the list is partitioned and you do not specify a partition name, all its partitions are exported.

partition_name

> Indicates that the export is a partition-level export. Partition-level export lets you export one or more specified partitions within a table. If this value is omitted for a partitioned table, all partitions will be exported.

TRANSPORTABLE_TABLESPACE = {Y | **N**}

> Allows the export of metadata for transportable tablespaces. Used in conjunction with the TABLESPACES parameter.

TRIGGERS = {**Y** | N}

> Causes triggers to be exported.

TTS_FULL_CHECK = {TRUE | **FALSE**}

> When this parameter is TRUE, Export makes sure that the tablespaces specified have no dependencies outside of the export.

Import-only parameters

The following parameters can be used only with the Import utility.

COMMIT = {Y | **N**}

> Specifies whether the import process should commit after each array insert. The default causes Import to commit after loading each table (if a table is partitioned, each partition in the export file is imported in a separate transaction). Specifying COMMIT=Y prevents rollback segments from growing too large. This setting is advisable if the table has a uniqueness constraint, because if the import is restarted, any rows that have already been imported are rejected with a nonfatal error. If a table does not have a uniqueness constraint and COMMIT=Y

---

is specified, Import could produce duplicate rows when the data is reimported.

COMPILE = {**Y** | N}
Specifies whether the import process should compile packages, procedures, and functions when they are imported.

DATAFILES = (*filename*[, *filename* ...])
When transportable tablespaces are used, this parameter gives a list of the datafiles that will be transported.

DESTROY = {Y | **N**}
Specifies whether existing datafiles making up the database should be reused if tablespaces are being re-created by Import.

WARNING

If datafiles are stored on a raw device, DESTROY=N does not prevent files from being overwritten.

FROMUSER = (*username*[, *username* ...])
Specifies a list of users whose schemas contain objects to import. The default for users without the IMP_FULL_DATABASE role is a user-mode import, in which objects for the current user are imported. If the specified user does not exist in the database, the objects will be imported into the schema of the current user unless TOUSER is also specified.

IGNORE = {Y | **N**}
Specifies how object creation errors are handled. The default causes Import not to import objects with creation errors (it will log and/or display the errors). If IGNORE=Y is specified, Import will import objects despite errors (and will not log errors).

INDEXFILE = *filename*
Specifies a file to receive table, index, and cluster creation commands. Table and cluster commands are included as

remarks but can be edited. *filename* is a common identifier, defined earlier. There is no default for this parameter, and it can be used only with the FULL=Y, FROMUSER, TOUSER, and/or TABLES parameters.

SHOW = {Y | **N**}

If SHOW=Y is specified, the SQL statements contained in the export file are listed to the display only, and objects are not imported. SHOW=Y can be used only with the FULL=Y, FROMUSER, TOUSER, and/or TABLES parameters.

TIP

You can use SHOW to regenerate Data Definition Language (DDL). Do an export, then do an import with SHOW=Y, redirecting the output to a file. Edit the file to get rid of messages that are not DDL, and you will have your DDL again.

SKIP_UNUSABLE_INDEXES = {Y | **N**}

Specifies whether Import skips building indexes set to the Index Unusable state. Without this parameter, row insertions that attempt to update unusable indexes fail.

STATISTICS = {**ALWAYS** | NONE | SAFE | RECALCULATE}

Specifies how optimize statistics should be handled by the import process.

ALWAYS

Specifies that statistics should always be imported, even if they are questionable.

NONE

Specifies that statistics are not to be imported nor calculated.

SAFE

> Specifies that statistics are to be imported only if they are not questionable; otherwise, recalculate statistics.

RECALCULATE

> Specifies that statistics are to be recalculated during import. This option is not valid if the export was performed with STATISTICS = NONE.

STREAMS_CONFIGURATION = {Y | **N**}

Specifies whether to import any general Streams-related metadata in the dump file.

STREAMS_INSTANTIATION = {Y | **N**}

Specifies whether to import any Streams instantiation metadata in the dump file.

TABLES = (*tablename*[, *tablename* ...])

Specifies that Import is to be run in table mode, and lists the table and partition names to be imported. There is no default. The *tablename* may be specified as *table:partition_name*, as follows; note that during import, table names cannot be qualified by a schema name.

table

> Indicates the name of a table to be imported. If a table in the list is partitioned and you do not specify a partition name, all its partitions are imported.

partition_name

> Indicates that the import is a partition-level import. Partition-level import lets you import one or more specified partitions within a table. If this value is omitted for a partitioned table, all partitions will be imported.

TOID_NOVALIDATE

Suppresses the validation of types with existing type IDs in the import database.

TOUSER = (*username*[, *username* …])

> Specifies a list of users whose schemas will be the target of the import. If multiple users are specified, the names must be paired with names in a corresponding FROMUSER parameter, such as:

```
FROMUSER=(tom,dick) TOUSER=(harry,dave)
```

TTS_OWNERS = (*ownername*[, *ownername* …])

> Specifies the owners of an imported transportable tablespace.

Data Pump Export and Import

The Data Pump Export and Import utilities were introduced with Oracle Database 10g Release 1. They have similar functionality and a similar look and feel to the original EXP and IMP utilities. However, files created by Data Pump Export are not compatible with files created by EXP; consequently, files created by EXP cannot be imported with Data Pump Import. Moreover, Oracle Database 10g features are fully supported only by Data Pump. For this reason—and because Data Pump provides improved performance—I recommend that you use the new Data Pump utilities if you are running Oracle Database10g.

Data Pump features

Data Pump Export and Import provide a variety of new backup and recovery features:

- You can specify the maximum number of threads of active execution operating on behalf of the Data Pump job, which allows the DBA to adjust resource consumption versus elapsed time. Note that this feature is available only with the Enterprise Edition for Oracle Database 10g.

- You can restart Data Pump jobs.

- You can detach from and reattach to long-running jobs without affecting the job itself. This allows DBAs and operations personnel to monitor jobs from multiple locations.

- Export and import operations can take place over a network; the source of each operation is a remote instance.
- In an import job, you can change the name of the source datafile to a different name in all DDL statements where the source datafile is referenced.
- Enhanced support is provided for remapping tablespaces during an import operation.
- You can filter the metadata that is exported and imported, based upon objects and object types.
- The programs provide an interactive-command mode that allows monitoring of and interaction with ongoing jobs.
- You can estimate how much space will be needed for an export without actually performing the export.
- You can specify the version of database objects to be moved.
- With Data Pump, export and import operations occur on the Oracle database server; in contrast, Original Import and Export were primarily client based.

There are a number of differences between the Data Pump programs and the Original Export and Import programs:

- The Data Pump programs operate on a group of files, called a *dump file set*, rather than on a single dump file.
- The Data Pump programs access files on the server rather than on the client; this means that directory objects are required when file locations are specified.
- The Data Pump programs use parallel execution rather than a single stream of execution, for improved performance; this means that the order of data within dump file sets is more variable.
- The Data Pump programs represent metadata in the dump file set as XML documents rather than as DDL commands.

- Tuning parameters that were used in Original Export and Import, such as BUFFER and RECORDLENGTH, are neither required nor supported by the Data Pump programs.

- With the Data Pump programs, it is not possible to perform interim commits during the restoration of a partition; this was provided by the COMMIT parameter in Original Import.

- With the Data Pump programs, there is no option to merge extents when you recreate tables. In Original Import, this was provided by the COMPRESS parameter. With Data Pump, extents are reallocated according to storage parameters for the target table.

- Sequential media, such as tapes and pipes, are not supported by the Data Pump programs.

- When importing data into an existing table using Data Pump, if any row violates an active constraint, the load is discontinued and no data is loaded; this is different from Original Import, which logs any rows that are in violation.

Data Pump privileges

To make full use of the Data Pump technology, you must be a privileged user. Privileged users (including those with the DBA role) have the EXP_FULL_DATABASE and IMP_FULL_DATABASE roles. Privileged users can do the following:

- Export and import database objects owned by others
- Export and import nonschema-based objects, such as tablespace and schema definitions, system privilege grants, resource plans, etc.
- Attach to, monitor, and control Data Pump jobs initiated by others
- Perform remapping operations on schemas and database datafiles

Data Pump Export and Import commands

You can run the Data Pump Export and Import utilities either interactively or via the command line. They are invoked interactively with the following commands:

```
EXPDP [username[/password][@service]]
IMPDP [username[/password][@service]]
```

In interactive mode, you can issue any of the following Export and Import commands:

ADD_FILE = [directory_object:]file_name[, ...]
  Available only with Data Pump Export. Adds more files or wildcard file templates to the export dump file set.

CONTINUE_CLIENT
  Changes the mode from interactive-command mode to logging mode. In logging mode, the job status is continually outputted to the terminal. If the job is currently stopped, then CONTINUE_CLIENT will also cause the client to attempt to start the job.

EXIT_CLIENT
  Stops the client session, exits, and discontinues logging to the terminal, but leaves the current job running. Because EXIT_CLIENT stops the client session but leaves the job running, you can attach to the job at a later time if it is still executing or in a stopped state.

HELP
  Displays information about the commands available in interactive-command mode.

KILL_JOB
  Detaches all currently attached client sessions and then kills the current job, exits, and returns to the terminal prompt. A job that is killed using KILL_JOB cannot be restarted.

PARALLEL = *integer*

> Dynamically specifies the number of active worker processes for the current job. PARALLEL is available as both a command-line parameter and an interactive-mode parameter.

START_JOB [= SKIP_CURRENT]

> Starts the current job to which you are attached. The job is restarted with no data loss or corruption after an unexpected failure or after you issue a STOP_JOB command, provided the dump file set and master table remain undisturbed. The SKIP_CURRENT option is valid only for Import jobs; it allows you to restart a job that previously failed to restart because execution of some DDL statement failed. The failing statement is skipped and the job is restarted from the next work item.

STATUS [= *integer*]

> Displays the cumulative status of the job, along with a description of the current operation. A completion percentage for the job is also returned. You have the option of specifying how frequently, in seconds, this status should be displayed in logging mode. If no value is entered or if 0 is specified, the periodic status display is turned off and the status is displayed only once.

STOP_JOB [= IMMEDIATE]

> Stops the current job either immediately or after an orderly shutdown, then exits Import. If the master table and dump file set are not disturbed when the STOP_JOB command is issued, the job can be attached to and restarted at a later time with the START_JOB command.

The command-line format for the Data Pump Export and Import utilities is:

```
EXPDP [username[/password][@service]]
      [parameter=value [parameter=value]...]
IMPDP [username[/password][@service]]
      [parameter=value [parameter=value]...]
```

The following parameters are available:

ATTACH [= [*schema_name.*]*job_name*]
    Attaches the client session to an existing job and automatically places you in the interactive-command interface.

CONTENT = {**ALL** | DATA_ONLY | METADATA_ONLY}
    Allows you to filter Export or Import. Specifies whether Data Pump operates on data only, metadata only, or both. The default exports or imports both data and metadata. DATA_ONLY exports or imports only table row data; no database object definitions are included. METADATA_ONLY exports or imports only database object definitions; no table row data is included.

DIRECTORY = *directory_object*
    Specifies the location to which Export writes the dump file set and the log file. The *directory_object* is the name of a database directory object (*not the name of an actual directory*) that was previously created by the DBA using the SQL CREATE DIRECTORY command.

DUMPFILE = [*directory_object:*]*file_name*[, ...]
    Specifies the names and, optionally, the directory objects of dump files for a job.

ESTIMATE = {**BLOCKS** | STATISTICS}
    For Export, specifies the method that will be used to estimate how much disk space each table in the export job will consume (in bytes). For Import, specifies the method that will be used to estimate the amount of data to be imported. The estimate is for table row data only; it does not include metadata. By default, the estimate is calculated by multiplying the number of database blocks that the target objects use by the appropriate block sizes. If you specify STATISTICS, the estimate is calculated using statistics for each table. The tables should have been analyzed recentlly.

ESTIMATE_ONLY = {Y | **N**}

Available only with Data Pump Export. Instructs Export to estimate the space that a job would consume (it does not actually perform the export operation).

EXCLUDE = *object_type*[:*name_clause*][, ...]

Enables you to filter the metadata that is exported or imported by specifying objects and object types that you want excluded from the operation. All object types for the given mode will be included except those specified in an EXCLUDE statement. If an object is excluded, all of its dependent objects are also excluded.

FILESIZE = *integer*[**B** | K | M | G]

This parameter, available only with Data Pump Export, specifies the maximum size (in bytes [the default], kilobytes, megabytes, or gigabytes) of each export dump file. The default is 0, which means unlimited.

FLASHBACK_SCN = *scn_value*

Specifies the SCN that will be used to enable the Flashback utility.

FLASHBACK_TIME = "TO_TIMESTAMP(*time_value*)"

Specifies that the SCN that most closely matches the specified time is to be found and used to enable the Flashback utility. The operation is performed with data that is consistent as of this SCN.

FULL = {Y | **N**}

Specifies that you want to perform a full database mode export or import. If FULL=Y, all data and metadata is included.

HELP = {Y | **N**}

Displays online help when Y is specified; no export or import is performed.

INCLUDE = *object_type*[:*name_clause*][, ...]

Enables you to filter the metadata that is exported or imported by specifying objects and object types for the

---

current mode. The specified objects and all their dependent objects are exported or imported. Only object types explicitly specified are included in the operation.

JOB_NAME = *jobname_string*
Specifies a name (up to 30 bytes) for the job. The job name is used to identify the job in subsequent actions, such as when the ATTACH parameter is used to attach to a job. The default is a system-generated name in the form SYS_*operation_mode*_NN.

LOGFILE = [*directory_object*:]*file_name*
Specifies the name and, optionally, a directory for the log file of the job.

NETWORK_LINK = *source_database_link*
Enables a network export or import when you specify the name of a valid database link.

NOLOGFILE = {Y | **N**}
Specifies whether to suppress creation of a log file.

PARALLEL = *integer*
Specifies the maximum number of threads of active execution operating on behalf of the export or import job. This execution set consists of a combination of worker processes and parallel I/O server processes. The default is 1.

PARFILE = [*directory_path*]*file_name*
Specifies the name of a parameter file, which can contain any Export or Import commands except another PARFILE command.

QUERY = [*schema*.][*table_name*:]*query_clause*
Enables you to filter the data that is exported or imported by specifying a clause for a SQL SELECT statement, which is applied to all tables in the job or to a specific table. The *query_clause* is typically a WHERE clause for fine-grained row selection, but could be any SQL clause.

REMAP_DATAFILE = *source_datafile:target_datafile*
Available only with Data Pump Import. Changes the name of the source datafile to the target datafile name in all SQL statements where the source datafile is referenced, which is useful when you move databases between platforms that have different filenaming conventions.

REMAP_SCHEMA = *source_schema:target_schema*
Available only with Data Pump Import. Loads all objects from the source schema into the target schema. If the schema you are remapping to does not already exist, the import operation creates it, provided the dump file set contains the necessary CREATE USER metadata and you are importing with enough privileges.

REMAP_TABLESPACE = *source_tablespace:target_tablespace*
Available only with Data Pump Import. Remaps all objects selected for import that have persistent data in the source tablespace that is to be created in the target tablespace. The target schema must have sufficient quota in the target tablespace.

REUSE_DATAFILES = {Y | **N**}
Available only with Data Pump Import. Specifies whether the import job should reuse existing datafiles for tablespace creation.

SCHEMAS = *schema_name*[, ...]
Specifies that you want to perform a schema-mode export or import. The default is the user's own schema.

SKIP_UNUSABLE_INDEXES = {Y | **N**}
Available only with Data Pump Import. Specifies whether Import skips loading tables that have indexes that were set to the Index Unusable state.

SQLFILE = [*directory_object*:]*file_name*
Available only with Data Pump Import. Specifies a file to record all of the SQL DDL that Import would execute, based on other parameters. The SQL is not actually executed, and the target system remains unchanged. If

directory_object is not explicitly specified, the file is written to the directory object specified in the DIRECTORY parameter.

STATUS = [*integer*]

Displays the detailed status of the job, a description of the current operation, and an estimated completion percentage for the job. Optionally, the status will be displayed every *integer* seconds in logging mode. Note that status information is written only to the standard output device, not to the log file.

STREAMS_CONFIGURATION={Y | N}

Available only with Data Pump Import. Specifies whether to import any general Streams metadata that may be present in the export dump file.

TABLE_EXISTS_ACTION = {SKIP | APPEND | TRUNCATE | REPLACE}

Available only with Data Pump Import. Specifies what Import should do if the table that it is trying to create already exists. The default is SKIP, unless CONTENT = DATA_ONLY is specified; in that case, the default is APPEND. The possible values are:

SKIP

Leaves the table as is and moves on to the next object. This is not a valid option if the CONTENT parameter is set to DATA_ONLY.

APPEND

Loads rows from the source and leaves existing rows unchanged.

TRUNCATE

Deletes existing rows and then loads rows from the source.

REPLACE

Drops the existing table and then creates and loads it from the source. This is not a valid option if the CONTENT parameter is set to DATA_ONLY.

TABLES = [*schema_name*.]*table_name*[:*partition_name*][, ...]
> Specifies that you want to perform a table-mode operation, and provides the name of one or more tables.

TABLESPACES = *tablespace_name*[, ...]
> Specifies a list of tablespace names to be exported or imported in tablespace mode.

TRANSFORM = {SEGMENT_ATTRIBUTES = {**Y** | N} | STORAGE = {**Y** | N}} [:{TABLE | INDEX}]
> Available only with Data Pump Import. Specifies that object creation DDL is to be altered for specific objects being loaded. If SEGMENT_ATTRIBUTES is specified as Y (the default), then segment attributes (physical attributes, storage attributes, tablespaces, and logging) are included, with appropriate DDL. If STORAGE is set to Y (the default), then storage clauses are included, with appropriate DDL. If TABLE or INDEX is supplied, the transform will apply to that.

TRANSPORT_DATAFILES = *datafile* [, *datafile* ...]
> Available only with Data Pump Import. Specifies one or more datafiles to be imported into the target database by a transportable-mode import.

TRANSPORT_FULL_CHECK = {Y | **N**}
> Specifies whether or not to check for dependencies between those objects inside the transportable set and those outside the transportable set. If Y is specified, then Export or Import verifies that there are no dependencies.

TRANSPORT_TABLESPACES = *tablespace* [, *tablespace* ...]
> Specifies that you want to perform a transportable-tablespace-mode export or import.

VERSION = {**COMPATIBLE** | LATEST | *version_string*}
> Specifies the version of database objects to be exported or imported. This can be used either to create a dump file set that is compatible with a previous release of Oracle, or to import data from a target system whose Oracle database is at an earlier version than that of the source

system. Database objects or attributes that are incompatible with the specified version will not be exported or imported. The values for this parameter are:

COMPATIBLE
> This is the default value. The version of the metadata corresponds to the database compatibility level. Database compatibility must be set to 9.2 or higher.

LATEST
> The version of the metadata corresponds to the database version.

version_string
> A specific database version (for example, 10.0.0). In Oracle Database 10g, this value cannot be lower than 9.2.

Export comparison

Table 2 compares Original Export and Data Pump Export parameters; note that in some cases, the names may be the same, but the functionality is slightly different.

Table 2. Comparison of Original Export and Data Pump Export parameters

Original Export	Data Pump Export
BUFFER	No corresponding parameter
COMPRESS	No corresponding parameter
CONSISTENT	No corresponding parameter; use FLASHBACK_SCN and FLASHBACK_TIME instead
CONSTRAINTS	EXCLUDE=CONSTRAINT and INCLUDE=CONSTRAINT
DIRECT	No corresponding parameter
FEEDBACK	STATUS
FILE	DUMPFILE
FILESIZE	FILESIZE
FLASHBACK_SCN	FLASHBACK_SCN
FLASHBACK_TIME	FLASHBACK_TIME

Table 2. Comparison of Original Export and Data Pump Export parameters (continued)

Original Export	Data Pump Export
FULL	FULL
GRANTS	EXCLUDE=GRANT and INCLUDE=GRANT
HELP	HELP
INCTYPE	No corresponding parameter
INDEXES	EXCLUDE=INDEX and INCLUDE=INDEX
LOG	LOGFILE
OBJECT_CONSISTENT	No corresponding parameter
OWNER	SCHEMAS
PARFILE	PARFILE
QUERY	QUERY
RECORDLENGTH	No corresponding parameter
RESUMABLE	No corresponding parameter
RESUMABLE_NAME	A parameter comparable to RESUMABLE_NAME is not needed; this functionality is provided automatically
RESUMABLE_TIMEOUT	No corresponding parameter
ROWS=N	CONTENT=METADATA_ONLY
ROWS=Y	CONTENT=ALL
STATISTICS	No corresponding parameter; statistics are always saved for tables
TABLES	TABLES
TABLESPACES	TABLESPACES (same parameter but slightly different behavior)
TRANSPORTABLE_TABLESPACE	TRANSPORT_TABLESPACES (same parameter but slightly different behavior)
TRIGGERS	EXCLUDE=TRIGGER and INCLUDE=TRIGGER
TTS_FULL_CHECK	TRANSPORT_FULL_CHECK
USERID	No corresponding parameter; this information is supplied as the username/password when you invoke Export
VOLSIZE	No corresponding parameter

Import comparison

Table 3 compares Original Import and Data Pump Import commands and parameters; note that in some cases, names may be the same, but the functionality is slightly different.

Table 3. Comparison of Original Import and Data Pump Import parameters

Original Import	Data Pump Import
BUFFER	No corresponding parameter
COMMIT	No corresponding parameter
COMPILE	No corresponding parameter
CONSTRAINTS	EXCLUDE=CONSTRAINT and INCLUDE=CONSTRAINT
DATAFILES	TRANSPORT_DATAFILES
DESTROY	REUSE_DATAFILES
FEEDBACK	STATUS
FILE	DUMPFILE
FILESIZE	No corresponding parameter
FROMUSER	SCHEMAS
FULL	FULL
GRANTS	EXCLUDE=GRANT and INCLUDE=GRANT
HELP	HELP
IGNORE	TABLE_EXISTS_ACTION
INDEXES	EXCLUDE=INDEX and INCLUDE=INDEX
INDEXFILE	SQLFILE
LOG	LOGFILE
PARFILE	PARFILE
RECORDLENGTH	No corresponding parameter
RESUMABLE	No corresponding parameter
RESUMABLE_NAME	No corresponding parameter
RESUMABLE_TIMEOUT	No corresponding parameter
ROWS=N	CONTENT=METADATA_ONLY

Original Import	Data Pump Import
ROWS=Y	CONTENT=ALL
SHOW	SQLFILE
SKIP_UNUSABLE_INDEXES	SKIP_UNUSABLE_INDEXES
STATISTICS	No corresponding parameter
STREAMS_CONFIGURATION	STREAMS_CONFIGURATION
STREAMS_INSTANTIATION	No corresponding parameter
TABLES	TABLES
TABLESPACES	This parameter still exists, but some of its functionality is now performed using the TRANSPORT_TABLESPACES parameter
TOID_NOVALIDATE	No corresponding parameter; OIDs are no longer used for type validation
TOUSER	REMAP_SCHEMA
TTS_OWNERS	No corresponding parameter
USERID	No corresponding parameter; this information is supplied as the username/password when you invoke Import
VOLSIZE	No corresponding parameter; tapes are no longer supported

User-Managed Backup and Recovery

It is possible to back up and recover a database using a combination of operating system commands. While automated recovery is fully supported by Oracle using the RMAN utility, many Oracle DBAs still prefer to manage backups directly.

Archivelog mode

When you run the database in archivelog mode, Oracle saves a copy of the redo logs into separate files called *offline redo logs.* Just as it uses the redo logs to perform the roll-forward process when restarting the database, Oracle can use the archive log files to replay transactions taken after a backup. Archive log files can be applied to either a hot backup or a cold backup.

What files should be backed up?

When performing a user-managed backup, you need to back up four types of files:

- Datafiles
- Log files
- Control files
- Miscellaneous files

Because you need all of these types of files for recovery operations, make sure that your user-managed backup routines include backups of all four file types.

Because your Oracle database is always changing, your first step in performing a user-managed backup is to determine the files you will need to back up. You can identify these files by running queries against the V$ views shown in Table 4.

Table 4. V$ views used in user-managed backup

Type of file/ V$ view	SQL
Datafile V$DATAFILE	SELECT NAME FROM V$DATAFILE
Online redo log files V$LOGFILE	SELECT MEMBER FROM V$LOGFILE;
Archived redo log files V$ARCHIVED_LOG	SELECT THREAD#, SEQUENCE#, NAME FROM V$ARCHIVED_LOG
Control file V$CONTROLFILE	SELECT NAME FROM V$CONTROLFILE;

Backing up datafiles

You can make a user-managed consistent backup of your complete Oracle database after you have shut it down with the NORMAL, IMMEDIATE, or TRANSACTIONAL keyword. Once the database is shut down, use the appropriate operating system command to back up or copy the datafiles.

You can also back up individual tablespaces and datafiles. If a tablespace is offline, use the appropriate operating system command to back up the datafiles. If the tablespace is online, you must first put the tablespace into backup mode by issuing the following command in SQL*Plus:

```
ALTER TABLESPACE tablespace_name BEGIN BACKUP;
```

Once the backup is complete, issue the following command to return to normal operation:

```
ALTER TABLESPACE tablespace_name END BACKUP;
```

Because there is extra overhead involved in writing the extra information to the log files while in backup mode, you should always end the mode as soon as your backup completes successfully.

NOTE

You may need to use the ALTER DATABASE END BACKUP command if your database is still in backup mode when it fails. Oracle will not reopen a tablespace in backup mode, so you will need to mount the database, run this command, and then open the database.

You may find that it makes more sense to back up your tablespaces serially, rather than in a single job. By backing up your tablespaces one at a time, you avoid having to put all the tablespaces in backup mode for the duration of the complete backup—instead, each tablespace is in backup mode only for the amount of time needed to back up that tablespace. This reduces the overall overhead of writing to the log files.

Backing up log files

If you are running in archivelog mode, your log files are being archived as soon as they are filled. The archiving process automatically backs up the filled log to another location. You may want to copy these archived files to backup media to protect against the possibility of media corruption.

Typically, you want to force the archiving of the current log after you have backed up your datafiles. To do this, execute the following command in SQL*Plus:

```
ALTER SYSTEM ARCHIVE LOG CURRENT;
```

Backing up the control file

The control file contains essential information about the current state of the database. You should always back up your control file when you make a user-managed backup (but not while the database is running). You can back up a control file in binary format to a binary location (by using the operating system's copy facility) or to a trace file. Backing up the control file to a binary location includes more information and is the method recommended by Oracle.

If you must back up the control file while the database is running, you can do so by executing the following command in SQL*Plus:

```
ALTER DATABASE BACKUP CONTROLFILE TO filename | TO TRACE
```

This backs up the control file to a trace file, which you can later use to recreate the control file with the CREATE CONTROLFILE command.

Backing up miscellaneous files

Other files, such as initialization files (*INIT.ORA* and *SPFILE*), networking parameter files (*TNSNAMES.ORA* and *LISTENER.ORA*), and password files, are an essential part of your Oracle environment. You should be sure to back up these files, either as a part of your normal user-managed backup or whenever they are changed.

Restoring datafiles

In the event of a media failure, you will have to use the files created with your user-managed backup to restore the database.

The restore process for datafiles has three basic steps: determining which datafiles need recovery, copying the relevant backup files, and then restoring the database to a workable state. The following sections describe these steps.

Determining the files to recover. If your control file has not been corrupted by the media failure, you can run the following command in SQL*Plus to obtain a list of the datafiles that need recovery:

```
SELECT * FROM V$RECOVER_FILE;
```

This query will return a set of numbers that indicates the files needing recovery. To determine which datafiles and tablespaces these file numbers represent, run the following command:

```
SELECT d.NAME, t.NAME AS Tablespace_Name
    FROM V$DATAFILE d, V$TABLESPACE
    WHERE d.TS# = t.TS# AND
    d.FILE# IN (filenumbers);
```

where *filenumbers* is a comma-separated list of the file numbers returned from the previous query.

Copying backup files. Once you have determined the datafiles that need recovery, you need to copy the backups of these files. To accomplish this, take the tablespace of each damaged datafile offline and copy the backup to the appropriate location.

If the media failure has made the default location unavailable, you will have to modify the control file to recognize the new location.

Restoring the database. Once the backup copy of the datafile has been copied, you must restore the tablespace that contains it. You can restore the database using SQL*Plus by following these steps:

1. Ensure that the database has been shut down:

   ```
   SHUTDOWN IMMEDIATE;
   ```

   or

   ```
   SHUTDOWN ABORT;
   ```

2. Copy your datafile from a good backup.

3. Start the database in mount mode:

   ```
   STARTUP MOUNT;
   ```

4. Recover the corrupt datafile through SQL*Plus:

   ```
   RECOVER TABLESPACE tablespace_name;
   ```

   or

   ```
   RECOVER DATAFILE datafile_name;
   ```

5. Open the database:

   ```
   ALTER DATABASE OPEN;
   ```

Restoring the control file

If you have specified multiple copies of your control file with the initialization parameter CONTROL_FILES, you can restore an individual copy of it by shutting down the database with the SHUTDOWN ABORT command; copying one of your other, undamaged control files to replace the damaged copy; and then bringing the database back up.

If a media failure has made the location of the damaged control file unavailable, follow the same procedure, but before bringing the database back up, edit the CONTROL_FILES initialization parameter to reflect the new location.

If you have to restore a single copy of a control file or if all copies of a multiplexed control file have been damaged, you must perform the following steps:

1. Shut down the database with the SHUTDOWN ABORT command.

2. Copy the backup of the control file to the appropriate location.

3. Mount the database with the STARTUP MOUNT command.

4. Issue the following command:

```
RECOVER DATABASE USING BACKUP CONTROLFILE;
```

5. Apply the archive log files as you are prompted to do so.

NOTE

If an archived log is not available, or if the recovery requires changes from the online redo log and it is not available, you will have to perform an incomplete recovery. To perform an incomplete recovery, add the keywords UNTIL CANCEL to the RECOVER command specified in the previous step.

---

6. Open the database and reset the log files with the following command:

```
ALTER DATABASE OPEN RESETLOGS;
```

After completing the recovery process, you should immediately perform a complete backup of your database.

Tablespace point-in-time recovery

Oracle provides another type of recovery operation known as *tablespace point-in-time recovery* (TSPITR). TSPITR is most commonly used with transportable tablespaces to recover from a variety of errors, such as mistakenly dropping a table or a tablespace, or encountering a logically corrupted table.

Transportable tablespaces provide an efficient way to move tablespaces from one database to another. You can simply copy the actual tablespace files, rather than having to back up and restore them or use Import and Export to move the data.

Follow these steps to perform a TSPITR:

1. Take the desired tablespaces offline in the original database.

2. Set up an auxiliary database.

3. Recover the tablespaces in the auxiliary database to the appropriate point in time.

4. Make the target tablespaces read-only in the auxiliary database.

5. Export the transportable tablespace information from the auxiliary database.

6. Drop the tablespaces in the original database.

7. Copy the tablespaces from the auxiliary database to the original database.

8. Import the transportable tablespace information into the original database.

9. Use transportable tablespaces to move the recovered tablespaces to the original database.

10. Enable read-write access for the new tablespaces.

Backup and Recovery Commands

The following section summarizes the syntax of the SQL commands used for backup and recovery. These commands are common to Oracle across all operating system platforms. Also included are two utilities that Oracle provides to allow you to test the validity of a backup (DBVERIFY) and to back up raw Windows partitions (OCOPY); for detailed information on these, see the Oracle documentation.

ALTER DATABASE BACKUP CONTROLFILE

Creates a backup of the current control file for the database.

```
ALTER DATABASE BACKUP CONTROLFILE TO filename | TO TRACE
```

to_filename
  Specifies the location of a copy of the current control file.

TO TRACE
  Causes the information in the control file to be written as SQL statements to a file in the database's trace directory. You can use this information to re-create the control file with the CREATE CONTROLFILE command.

ALTER DATABASE OPEN

Opens the database after performing user-managed recovery.

```
ALTER DATABASE OPEN dbname [NORESETLOGS | RESETLOGS]
```

dbname
    Specifies the name of the database to be opened.

NORESETLOGS
    Continues numbering the archive logs from the last set. This is the default value and is used after a complete recovery of the database.

RESETLOGS
    Needed after incomplete recovery or use of a backup control file to ensure that old archived logs are not used to recover the new incarnation of the database. After this step, the database loses all memory of the previous backups.

ALTER SYSTEM

Suspends or resumes I/O operations.

```
ALTER SYSTEM {SUSPEND | RESUME}
```

If SUSPEND is specified, ALTER SYSTEM suspends all I/O operations to the database to accommodate third-party products that require this type of pause—for example, to break a mirror. Be sure to put the relevant tablespaces in backup mode before you suspend I/O and take them back out of backup mode after you resume I/O operations (using RESUME).

CREATE CONTROLFILE

Allows you to recreate the control file.

```
CREATE CONTROLFILE [REUSE] [SET]
    DATABASE database_name
    [LOGFILE {[GROUP integer] filename} ...]
    [RESETLOGS | NORESETLOGS]
    [DATAFILE filename]
    [MAXLOGFILES integer]
    [MAXLOGMEMBERS integer]
    [MAXLOGHISTORY integer]
```

```
[MAXDATAFILES integer]
[MAXINSTANCES integer]
[ARCHIVELOG | NOARCHIVELOG]
[CHARACTER SET character_set]
```

This is a SQL*Plus command. You can create the control file by manually entering the values for the control file or by using the text file created with a previous BACKUP CONTROLFILE TO TRACE command.

REUSE
> Causes the control file named in the CONTROL_FILE initialization parameter to become the new control file. If the control file named in the initialization file exists and the REUSE keyword is not used, an error will be returned.

SET
> Indicates that the *database_name* is the new name for the database.

DATABASE *database_name*
> Specifies the name of the database for the control file.

LOGFILE *filename*
> Specifies the name of the log file to be used for the database. You must list all members of all redo log groups.

GROUP *integer*
> Specifies the number of the log file group.

RESETLOGS | NORESETLOGS
> Indicates whether the database should ignore any log files listed for the log file clause. These keywords are used to prevent log file conflicts in the event of an incomplete recovery.

DATAFILE *filename*
> Specifies the datafiles for the database. You must list all datafiles for the database.

MAXLOGFILES *integer*
> Specifies the maximum number of log files that can ever be created for the database.

MAXLOGMEMBERS *integer*
> Specifies the maximum number of members for a redo log file. A member is an identical copy of a redo log file.

MAXLOGHISTORY *integer*
    Specifies the maximum number of archived redo log file
    groups for automatic media recovery with Real Application
    Clusters or Oracle Parallel Server.

MAXDATAFILES *integer*
    Specifies the maximum number of datafiles used initially for
    the database; this value is used to size the datafile section of
    the control file.

MAXINSTANCES *integer*
    Specifies the maximum number of instances that can have the
    database simultaneously mounted and open.

ARCHIVELOG | **NOARCHIVELOG**
    Indicates whether the database will be in archivelog mode.

CHARACTER SET *character_set*
    Specifies the character set that is reconstructed in the control
    file, where it can be used to properly interpret the tablespace
    names for the database.

DBVERIFY

Tests the validity of your backup.

```
DBV FILE=filename
```

This is an Oracle utility command; *filename* is the name of the
backup file to be verified.

OCOPY

Backs up raw partitions on Windows systems.

```
OCOPY from_rawfile to_file |
OCOPY /b from_file to_drive |
OCOPY /r from_drive to_rawfile |
```

This is an Oracle utility command.

from_rawfile
    Filename of the raw partition.

to_file
    Filename to receive the backup of the raw partition.

/b
> Indicates that Oracle is to back up a raw partition to span multiple copies of media on a drive, such as a disk drive.

from_file
> Filename of the raw partition.

to_drive
> Drive to receive the backup of the raw partition.

/r
> Specifies recovery of a raw partition that has been backed up to multiple copies of media, such as a disk drive.

from_drive
> Drive that will contain the multiple copies of media.

to_rawfile
> Name of the raw partition that will be restored using the information from the multiple copies of media.

RECOVER

Restores a database.

```
RECOVER {general_clause | managed_clause | END BACKUP}

general_clause :=
[AUTOMATIC] [FROM location]
    {{full_database_recovery_options |
    partial_database_recovery_options |
    LOGFILE filename}
    {[TEST | ALLOW integer CORRUPTION]} ... |
    CONTINUE [DEFAULT] | CANCEL}
    [PARALLEL [integer]]

full_database_recovery_options :=
[STANDBY] DATABASE
    [{UNTIL {CANCEL | TIME date | CHANGE integer} |
    USING BACKUP CONTROLFILE]

partial_database_recovery_options :=
TABLESPACE tablespace_name [, tablespace_name] ... |
    DATAFILE datafile_name [, datafile_name] ... |
    STANDBY {TABLESPACE tablespace_name
        [, tablespace_ name] ... |
        DATAFILE datafile_name [, datafile_name] ...}
        UNTIL [CONSISTENT WITH] CONTROLFILE
```

```
managed_clause :=
MANAGED STANDBY DATABASE
   [{NODELAY | [TIMEOUT] integer | CANCEL [IMMEDIATE
       [NOWAIT]} |
   [DISCONNECT [FROM SESSION]] [FINISH [NOWAIT]]]
```

RECOVER applies the appropriate log files to a datafile to restore the database. This operation rolls forward the transactions from the logs and then rolls back the uncommitted transactions. Note that you can use the RECOVER option of the SQL ALTER DATABASE command to perform the same operations.

END BACKUP
   Takes the database out of online backup mode.

AUTOMATIC
   Causes the name of the next archived redo file to be automatically generated, based on the LOG_ARCHIVE_DEST and LOG_ARCHIVE_FORMAT parameters. If no file matching the automatically generated name exists, SQL*Plus prompts you for the name of the file. This functionality can also be implemented with the SET AUTORECOVERY ON statement.

FROM location
   The location of the archived log file group. If this parameter is missing, SQL*Plus uses the value specified in the LOG_ARCHIVE_DEST initialization parameter.

LOGFILE filename
   Specifies the name of the log file to be used for recovery.

TEST
   Lets you run a trial recovery to determine if there are problems with the files that will be used in the recovery process. A trial recovery reads through the required files but does not write the specified changes to disk.

ALLOW integer CORRUPTION
   Specifies how many corrupt blocks can be found without canceling the entire recovery or trial recovery process.

CONTINUE
   Used to continue multi-instance recovery after the process has been interrupted to disable a thread.

CONTINUE DEFAULT
Indicates that recovery should continue with automatically generated archived log file names.

CANCEL
Cancels the current recovery process.

PARALLEL [integer]
Allows recovery to continue in parallel. This option may not help in all situations—for example, if the I/O bottleneck is in the actual disk hardware. If you do not specify an integer, Oracle will calculate the degree of parallelism using the number of CPUs and the PARALLEL_THREADS_PER_CPU initialization parameter.

DATABASE
Recovers the entire database.

STANDBY DATABASE
Recovers the standby database with the control file and archived log files.

UNTIL CANCEL | TIME | CHANGE
Causes the recovery process to continue until you enter ALTER DATABASE RECOVER CANCEL, until a specified time, or until a specified SCN number. There is no default.

USING BACKUP CONTROLFILE
Specifies that recovery is to be performed using a backup control file instead of the current control file.

TABLESPACE
Follow this keyword with the name of the tablespace(s) you want to recover.

STANDBY TABLESPACE
Specifies that a lost or damaged tablespace in the standby database is to be reconstructed using archived redo log files from the primary database and from a control file.

DATAFILE
Follow this keyword with the name of the datafile(s) that you want to recover.

UNTIL CONSISTENT WITH CONTROLFILE
Specifies that the recovery should continue until the datafile or tablespace is consistent with the current standby database control file.

MANAGED STANDBY DATABASE
Starts automated standby recovery mode.

NODELAY
Overrides any DELAY setting to immediately apply an archived log file to the standby database.

TIMEOUT *integer*
Specifies the time in minutes a managed recovery operation will wait for an archived log file. If this time is exceeded, the recovery operation terminates and you must reissue the RECOVER command to restart the managed recovery operation.

CANCEL
Terminates the managed recovery operation and returns session control after the recovery process terminates.

CANCEL IMMEDIATE
Terminates the managed recovery operation after applying all redo information in the current log or after the next log file read. Session control returns after the recovery process has terminated.

CANCEL IMMEDIATE NOWAIT
Like CANCEL IMMEDIATE, but session control returns immediately.

CANCEL NOWAIT
Cancels the managed recovery operation after the next log file read and returns control to the session immediately.

DISCONNECT [FROM SESSION]
Runs the managed recovery operation as a background process.

FINISH
Causes the managed recovery process to recover the current log files of the standby database. When used with the NOWAIT keyword, returns control immediately to the session.

STARTUP MOUNT

Mounts the database (identified by *dbname*) but does not open it. Strictly speaking, STARTUP MOUNT is not a SQL statement, but it is issued from SQL*Plus.

```
STARTUP MOUNT dbname
```

You must use this command to perform a user-managed recovery operation.

Recovery Manager

RMAN is a facility provided by Oracle to manage hot and cold backups and the associated archive files.

WARNING

RMAN provides support only for hot and cold backups. It does not support exports or imports.

RMAN maintains a separate recovery database of all files necessary to recreate the Oracle database as it was at a particular point in time. It also maintains information about the location of the files. RMAN also allows you to perform incremental hot backups. It is able to look at each data block, determine whether it has changed since the time of the last backup, and write out only those blocks that have changed. This feature can significantly reduce the amount of time and storage required to back up a large database.

While RMAN helps automate the recovery process, you are not required to use it. DBAs have been successfully backing up and restoring databases without RMAN for years. There are also several third-party tools available that provide support for backing up databases.

Although many of RMAN's operations can be performed with the other methods previously described, RMAN provides some significant advantages over user-managed backup and recovery, including:

- Performing a backup without having to put the database in backup mode
- Performing an incremental backup of only those data blocks that have changed
- Automatically tracking and logging backup operations
- Automatically detecting block corruption during backup
- Reporting on backup operations
- Performing block media recovery

RMAN fundamentals

Oracle uses some specific terminology in describing RMAN operations that may differ from terms used in other forms of backup and recovery:

Server processes
> RMAN uses a number of server processes to operate. These server processes are started whenever you start RMAN or use one of its features—for example, when you connect to a catalog or allocate a channel for backup.

Channel
> A *channel* is an RMAN server process that communicates with a particular backup device. You must allocate a channel before you can begin any backup operations.

Target and catalog
> RMAN can interact with two different Oracle databases. The *target* database is the database for which you are performing backup or recovery operations. The *catalog* is a database that acts as a repository for information about

RMAN activities. The catalog is normally another Oracle database on a different Oracle host; using a different host prevents a failure on the main host from destroying the very catalog information that will be needed to recover from that failure.

The catalog includes a specific schema that will hold the relevant information. To create a catalog for RMAN, you first connect to the catalog database with RMAN and issue the CREATE CATALOG command. If you want to use a catalog for RMAN, you must first register any target databases using RMAN's REGISTER command in order for those databases to use the catalog.

You don't have to use a catalog, because RMAN includes information about any backup in the target database's control files. However, the catalog gives you more management flexibility by maintaining a greater amount of historical data about all the backups done on a database.

Media Management Layer

If you will be using a tape drive for your RMAN backups, you will have to use a Media Management Layer (MML) to communicate with the tape drive. The MML is third-party software that generally comes from the hardware vendor.

Backup sets

Whenever you create a backup with RMAN, you are actually creating one or more *backup sets*. A backup set is a logical entity composed of one or more physical *backup pieces*, the physical files that make up a backup set. Datafiles and control files can be in the same backup set, but archived log files must be in a different backup set. The only way to restore a database from backup pieces is through RMAN.

Running RMAN

In order to run RMAN, you must have SYSDBA privileges, either through operating system authentication or by use of a password file. If you are using OS authentication, you must also properly establish the following target environment variables:

> ORACLE_SID
> ORACLE_HOME

To run RMAN, type the following at the command prompt:

> `> RMAN [option[ option ...]]`

RMAN will display the RMAN> prompt.

You can connect to a target database and a recovery catalog within RMAN by issuing the CONNECT command.

You can specify the following options when invoking the RMAN executable:

APPEND
> Indicates that RMAN should append new messages onto the end of the existing message file. If you do not specify this keyword and the log file has the name of a file that already exists, the existing file is overwritten.

AUXILARY
> Specifies a string containing the connect string for the recovery catalog database. Auxiliary databases are used to create duplicate standby databases (using the DUPLICATE command) or to implement tablespace point-in-time recovery.

CATALOG | **NOCATALOG**
> Specifies a string containing the connect string for the recovery catalog database. If you do not specify a recovery catalog when you connect or within RMAN, backup operations will proceed without a catalog. NOCATALOG indicates that RMAN will not start with a particular recovery catalog.

CMDFILE
Specifies a string containing the name of a file containing RMAN commands. Once the commands in the file have completed, RMAN terminates.

DEBUG
Activates debug mode for RMAN, which produces verbose messages for each RMAN command. You can specify the type and level of debug messages produced.

LOG
Specifies a string containing the path and filename for the output message log file.

MSGNO
Causes the RMAN message number to be included in all output from commands.

PIPE
Specifies a string containing the name of a pipe that can be used to pass commands to RMAN. Pipes can be used in conjunction with the Oracle built-in package DBMS_PIPE.

SEND
Specifies a string containing a command that is sent to the destinations of all allocated channels. Support of this feature is provided by the MML for a particular device.

TARGET
Specifies a string containing the connect string for the target database. If you do not include a connect string, RMAN connects to the Oracle database specified by the ORACLE_SID environment variable.

TIMEOUT
Specifies the amount of time (in seconds) that a pipe will wait for input. If this time limit is exceeded, RMAN will terminate.

TRACE
Specifies a string containing the path and filename of the output debug message file.

Using RMAN scripts

When you specify the backup or recovery operations to be performed by RMAN, you will frequently need to include several commands. If you make a mistake entering one of these commands, RMAN will abort the entire job. Because of this behavior, many DBAs use scripts containing a verified set of RMAN commands.

NOTE

You may want to create operating system scripts containing all the commands needed to run an RMAN job, from setting the environment variables to actually backing up or restoring the database. You may also want to create operating system scripts that pass variables to RMAN. The syntax for these scripts is the standard syntax for scripts for your operating system.

You can also create scripts to run within RMAN. The @ command calls an operating system script from within RMAN. The @@ command calls another script from within a called script (both scripts must be in the same directory).

You can store scripts in the recovery catalog with the following command in RMAN:

```
RMAN> CREATE SCRIPT script_name {scriptbody}
```

To edit an existing script, use the same syntax, but begin with the keywords REPLACE SCRIPT.

You can run a script stored in the catalog using the command:

```
RMAN> RUN {EXECUTE SCRIPT script_name;}
```

You can delete a script from the catalog as follows:

```
RMAN> DELETE SCRIPT script_name;
```

You can view a script stored in the catalog in two ways. You can use RMAN's PRINT command followed by the script name, or you can query the actual tables used to store the

---

script. The following SQL query on the catalog database will retrieve all the scripts stored in the database:

```
SELECT a.script_name, a.text
    FROM rc_stored_script_line a, rc_stored_script b
    WHERE a.db_key = b.db_key
```

In addition to providing commands that shape the operation of your Oracle database, RMAN allows you to call any SQL statement from its prompt. To do so, type the SQL statement followed by a quoted string containing the SQL syntax.

RMAN commands

The main purpose of RMAN is to make it easy to perform backup and recovery operations. The command needed to do a full online backup of your database is quite simple. The following examples assume that you have already connected to the target database and that you are using defaults for all options.

```
RMAN> BACKUP DATABASE FORMAT
2> '/d99/rmanback/brdstn/rman_%d_%t_%U.bus';
```

To perform a normal recovery operation with RMAN, use the following commands, assuming that the database is already closed:

```
RMAN> RESTORE DATABASE;
RMAN> RECOVER DATABASE;
RMAN> ALTER DATABASE OPEN;
```

RMAN provides a lot of flexibility for shaping the way you perform backup and recovery operations. As a result, there are too many RMAN commands and parameters to fit in this book. Two good sources of detailed information about these commands and parameters are the *RMAN Pocket Reference* and *Oracle in a Nutshell*, both from O'Reilly.

Security

Oracle provides a variety of features that can help secure your database from unauthorized access and can help protect your data from being seen or manipulated by unauthorized users. This section provides information on Oracle's major security features: authentication, profiles, privileges, roles, and auditing.

Authentication

Authentication is the process of identifying and recognizing authorized users of the database. Oracle security is primarily based on the concept of individual authorized users, so authentication is a critical component.

Two system users are created when you install Oracle:

SYS
> The schema for SYS contains the base tables and views used for the data dictionary. You should never change any of these tables. The SYS user has the DBA role. (Roles are described in the "Roles" section later in this book.) The default password for SYS is CHANGE_ON_INSTALL.

SYSTEM
> The SYSTEM username is used to create additional tables and views for administrative information. The SYSTEM user has the DBA role. The default password for SYSTEM is MANAGER.

When you create an Oracle database using the CREATE DATABASE statement, you can use the USER SYS IDENTIFIED BY *password* and USER SYSTEM IDENTIFIED BY *password* clauses to protect access by these powerful pre-created users.

In addition to SYS and SYSTEM, users can be created with the CREATE USER command. User characteristics can be modified with the ALTER USER command. Both commands are described below.

CREATE USER

Creates a user and specifies basic characteristics of the user.

```
CREATE USER username
    IDENTIFIED {BY password | EXTERNALLY |
        GLOBALLY AS 'external_name'}
    [DEFAULT TABLESPACE tablespace_name]
    [TEMPORARY TABLESPACE tablespace_name]
    [QUOTA {integer (K | M) | UNLIMITED} ON
        tablespace_name] ...
    [PROFILE profilename]
    [PASSWORD EXPIRE]
    [ACCOUNT LOCK | UNLOCK]
```

IDENTIFIED BY
> Specifies the way the user will be authenticated. There are three options for authentication (there is no default):

password
> Identified with a locally stored password. The password can contain only single-byte characters from the database character set.

EXTERNALLY
> Identified by an external service, such as the operating system. If you want the user to have access only through the operating system account, add the OS_AUTHENT_ PREFIX parameter value before the username.

GLOBALLY AS 'external_name'
> Identified by an enterprise directory service. The external_name can be either the Distinguished Name from the directory or NULL, which indicates that the directory will map users to the appropriate database schema.

DEFAULT TABLESPACE
> Specifies the default tablespace for objects created by the user. The default is the SYSTEM tablespace.

TEMPORARY TABLESPACE
    Specifies the tablespace used for the user's temporary storage.
    The default is the SYSTEM tablespace.

QUOTA
    Specifies the amount of space the user can use in the speci-
    fied tablespace. You can have multiple QUOTA clauses for
    multiple tablespaces. You can specify kilobytes (K) or mega-
    bytes (M). UNLIMITED means the user will have no
    restrictions on space usage.

PROFILE
    Specifies the profile assigned to the user. For more informa-
    tion, see the "Profiles" section later in this book.

PASSWORD EXPIRE
    Specifies that the user or the DBA will have to change the
    user's password before the user can log in to the database.

ACCOUNT LOCK | **UNLOCK**
    Disables or enables access through the user account.

ALTER USER

Changes the characteristics of an existing user.

```
ALTER USER username
    [IDENTIFIED {BY password [REPLACE old_password]
        EXTERNALLY | GLOBALLY AS 'external_name'}]
    [DEFAULT TABLESPACE tablespace_name]
    [TEMPORARY TABLESPACE tablespace_name]
    [QUOTA {integer [K | M] | UNLIMITED} ON
        tablespace_ name] ...
    [PROFILE profile_name]
    [DEFAULT ROLE {[role_name[,role_name ...] |
        ALL {EXCEPT [role_name[, role_name ...]]} | NONE
    [PASSWORD EXPIRE]
    [ACCOUNT LOCK | UNLOCK]
    [username [,username ...] proxy_clause]
```

Most keywords for the ALTER USER command have the same
meaning as those specified for CREATE USER. The following
keywords apply only to ALTER USER:

REPLACE *old_password*
> If the password complexity verification function is turned on, you must specify your old password when you change it with the ALTER USER command.

DEFAULT ROLE
> A role is a way to manage groups of user privileges for groups of users. You can specify multiple roles for a user; ALL or ALL EXCEPT roles for a user; or no role for a user. For more information on roles, see the "Roles" section later in this book.

proxy_clause
> The proxy clause can be used with more than one user's name. In Oracle Database 10g and Oracle9i Database, the user identity, in the form of a Distinguished Name or a full X.509 certificate, can be passed to the database for identification without reauthentication.

> The proxy clause has the following syntax:

```
{GRANT | REVOKE} CONNECT THROUGH proxy
    [WITH {ROLE [role_name[, role_name ...]] |
        ALL [EXCEPT] [role_name[, role_name ...]] |
        NO ROLES}]
    AUTHENTICATED USING {PASSWORD |
        DISTINGUISHED NAME | CERTIFICATE
        [TYPE 'type_name'][VERSION 'version_ name']}
```

GRANT | REVOKE
> Allows or prohibits the proxy connection.

CONNECT THROUGH *proxy*
> Identifies the proxy connecting to Oracle.

WITH ROLE
> Assigns a role to the proxy user. The syntax is the same as for the DEFAULT ROLE keyword.

AUTHENTICATED USING
> Specifies if the proxy will be authenticated by a source other than the proxy. The DISTINGUISHED NAME and CERTIFICATE indicate that the proxy is acting on behalf of a global database user. There is no default.

Profiles

A *profile* can be associated with a user to control the resources available to that user or to specify a condition on how passwords are administered. By limiting the computing resources that an individual can use, the DBA can prevent any single user from exhausting resources and affecting other users. By placing limits on how passwords are administered, the DBA can help to safeguard the authentication process for the Oracle database.

In order to use profiles, the DBA must enable dynamic resource limits with either the RESOURCE_LIMIT initialization parameter or the ALTER SYSTEM SET command. Commands related to profiles are described below.

CREATE PROFILE

Allows the DBA to create a profile and assign different types of resource limits to the profile.

```
CREATE PROFILE profile_name LIMIT
    {resource_parameter | password_parameter}
```

The following values can be used for both resource and password parameters, unless specified otherwise in the descriptions:

UNLIMITED
Specifies no limit for the particular parameter.

DEFAULT
Specifies that the parameter assumes the value specified for the DEFAULT profile. Initially, all values for the DEFAULT profile are specified as UNLIMITED. You can change the values for the DEFAULT profile with the ALTER PROFILE command.

resource_parameter | *password_parameter*
For resource parameters, the value is an integer. For password parameters, the value is an expression.

Resource Parameters Only

Except as noted, if a user attempts to perform an operation that exceeds any of the resource limits, Oracle aborts the operation, rolls back the current statement, returns an error, and leaves the transaction intact.

SESSIONS_PER_USER
> Limits the number of concurrent sessions for the user.

CPU_PER_SESSION
> Limits the CPU time for a user session, in hundredths of seconds.

CPU_PER_CALL
> Limits the CPU time for an individual call by the user, in hundredths of seconds.

CONNECT_TIME
> Limits the total elapsed time for a session for the user, in minutes. If a user exceeds this parameter, Oracle rolls back the current transaction and ends the session. The next call made by the user will return an error.

IDLE_TIME
> Limits the amount of continuous idle time for the user, in minutes. Idle time does not apply to long-running queries or other operations. If a user exceeds this parameter, Oracle rolls back the current transaction and ends the session. The next call made by the user will return an error.

LOGICAL_READS_PER_SESSION
> Limits the number of logical data blocks read in a user's session, from either memory or disk.

LOGICAL_READS_PER_CALL
> Limits the number of logical data blocks read in for each call by the user, from either memory or disk.

COMPOSITE_LIMIT
> Limits the total resource cost of a session, as a number of service units. Oracle calculates service units as a weighted sum of these initialization parameters: CPU_PER_SESSION, CONNECT_TIME, LOGICAL_READS_PER_ SESSION, and PRIVATE_SGA. You can modify the weight given to each of these resources with the ALTER RESOURCE COST command.

PRIVATE_SGA {*integer* {K | M} | UNLIMITED | DEFAULT}
  Limits the amount of private space a user's session can allocate from the shared pool of the SGA, in kilobytes (K) or megabytes (M).

Password Parameters Only

FAILED_LOGIN_ATTEMPTS
  Sets a limit on the number of failed login attempts a user is allowed before the account is locked.

PASSWORD_LIFE_TIME
  Sets a limit on the maximum time a single password can be used by the user, in days. At the end of this time, the password expires.

PASSWORD_REUSE_TIME
  Specifies how many days must pass before a password can be reused. If you use an integer value for this parameter, you must set the PASSWORD_REUSE_MAX parameter to UNLIMITED.

PASSWORD_REUSE_MAX
  Specifies the number of password changes before a previous password can be reused. If you use an integer value for this parameter, you must set the PASSWORD_REUSE_TIME parameter to UNLIMITED.

PASSWORD_LOCK_TIME
  Specifies the number of days a user's account will be locked if the number of login attempts is exceeded.

PASSWORD_GRACE_TIME
  Specifies the number of days a warning is issued prior to a password's expiring.

PASSWORD_VERIFY_FUNCTION {*function* | NULL | DEFAULT}
  Allows the use of a PL/SQL function to verify password complexity.

ALTER PROFILE

Changes the resource or parameter limits for an existing profile.

```
ALTER PROFILE profile_name LIMIT
    {resource_parameter | password_parameter}
```

The ALTER PROFILE command uses the same keywords and values as those specified for CREATE PROFILE .

DROP PROFILE

Deletes an existing profile.

```
DROP PROFILE profile_name [CASCADE]
```

If CASCADE is specified, the profile will be desassigned from any active users and replaced with the DEFAULT profile. You must use this clause to drop a profile for a currently active user.

Privileges

A *privilege* is a right that is assigned to an individual user or role. There are two basic types of privileges:

- System privileges give the user or role the ability to perform certain system operations.
- Schema object privileges give the user or role access privileges on individual schema objects.

System privileges relate to the Oracle instance as a whole (for example, a privilege on all of a given type of object, such as all tables), while schema privileges relate to a specific schema object within an Oracle database (for example, a particular table).

System privileges

The following list describes privileges that apply to many Oracle system privilege types.

ANY
> Gives the privilege to perform the action on objects in any schema. Without this keyword, a privilege is granted only on objects within the user's schema. By default, the ANY keyword gives the user privileges on all objects in all schemas, including the SYS schema. To prevent access to the SYS schema with the ANY privilege, you can set the O7_DICTIONARY_ACCESSIBILITY initialization parameter to FALSE.

ALTER
Gives the privilege to alter the type of object.

CREATE
Gives the privilege to create the type of object.

DROP
Gives the privilege to drop the type of object.

EXECUTE
Gives the privilege to execute or reference the type of object.

SELECT ANY
Gives the privilege to access objects. Because users always have the ability to access objects in their own schema, SELECT ANY always includes the ANY keyword.

In each of the privilege entries below, there are two categories of privileges: unique (those that apply only to that particular privilege type) and common (those in the above list, which apply to many different types of privileges).

AUDIT

Allows auditing functions. The unique privilege is:

AUDIT SYSTEM
Gives the privilege to issue AUDIT commands in SQL.

The only common privilege is ANY.

CLUSTER

Provides the ability to work with clusters. There are no unique privileges. The common privileges are CREATE [ANY], ALTER ANY, and DROP ANY.

CONTEXT

Provides the ability to work with contexts. There are no unique privileges. Common privileges are CREATE ANY and DROP ANY.

DATABASE

Provides the ability to use the ALTER DATABASE command. There are no unique privileges. The only common privilege is ALTER.

DATABASE LINKS

Provides the ability to work with database links. Unique privileges are:

CREATE PUBLIC
>   Gives the privilege to create public database links.

DROP PUBLIC
>   Gives the privilege to drop public database links.

The only common privilege is CREATE.

DEBUG

Provides the ability to work with the debugger. Unique privileges are:

DEBUG CONNECT SESSION
>   Gives the privilege to connect the current session to a debugger that uses the Java Debug Wire Protocol.

DEBUG ANY PROCEDURE
>   Gives the privilege to debug any PL/SQL and Java code in any database object, as well as to display all SQL statements executed by the application.

There are no common privileges.

DIMENSION

Provides the ability to work with dimensions. There are no unique privileges. Common privileges are CREATE [ANY], ALTER ANY, and DROP ANY.

DIRECTORY

Provides the ability to work with directories. There are no unique privileges. Common privileges are CREATE ANY and DROP ANY.

INDEX

Provides the ability to work with indexes. For unique privileges, see the entry for [GLOBAL] QUERY REWRITE under "Miscellaneous privileges" later in this section. Common privileges are CREATE ANY, ALTER ANY, and DROP ANY.

INDEXTYPE

Provides the ability to work with user-created index types. There are no unique privileges. Common privileges are CREATE [ANY], ALTER ANY, DROP ANY, and EXECUTE ANY.

LIBRARY

Provides the ability to work with libraries. There are no unique privileges. Common privileges are CREATE [ANY] and DROP ANY.

MATERIALIZED VIEW

Provides the ability to work with materialized views. Materialized views are preaggregated summaries used for business intelligence operations. For unique privileges, see the entries for [GLOBAL] QUERY REWRITE and FLASHBACK ANY TABLE under "Miscellaneous privileges," later in this section. In addition, the following is supported:

ON COMMIT REFRESH
> Gives the privilege to create a materialized view that is refreshed on COMMITs.

Common privileges are CREATE [ANY], ALTER ANY, and DROP ANY.

OPERATOR

Provides the ability to work with user-defined operators. There are no unique privileges. Common privileges are CREATE [ANY], DROP, and EXECUTE.

OUTLINE

Provides the ability to work with stored outlines. The only unique privilege is:

SELECT ANY
Although this uses a common keyword for objects, these keywords give the privilege to create a private outline from a public outline.

Common privileges are CREATE ANY, ALTER ANY, and DROP ANY.

PROCEDURE

Provides the ability to work with procedures. There are no unique privileges. Common privileges are CREATE [ANY], ALTER ANY, DROP ANY, and EXECUTE ANY.

PROFILE

Provides the ability to work with profiles. There are no unique privileges. Common privileges are CREATE, ALTER, and DROP.

RESOURCE COST

Provides the ability to assign costs to resources. There are no unique privileges. The only common privileges is ALTER.

ROLE

Provides the ability to work with roles. The only unique privilege is:

GRANT ANY
Gives the privilege to grant any role in the database.

Common privileges are CREATE, ALTER ANY, and DROP ANY.

ROLLBACK SEGMENT

Provides the ability to work with rollback segments. There are no unique privileges. Common privileges are CREATE, ALTER, and DROP.

SEQUENCE

Provides the ability to work with sequences. There are no unique privileges. Common privileges are CREATE [ANY], ALTER ANY, DROP ANY, and SELECT ANY.

SESSION

Provides the ability to work with sessions. Unique privileges are:

ALTER RESOURCE COST
    Gives the privilege to set the costs for session resources.

RESTRICTED SESSION
    Gives the privilege to log on after the Oracle instance is started with the STARTUP RESTRICT command.

Common privileges are CREATE and ALTER.

SYNONYM

Provides the ability to work with synonyms. There are no unique privileges. Common privileges are CREATE [ANY] [PUBLIC], DROP ANY, and DROP PUBLIC.

SYSTEM

Provides the ability to alter system parameters. There are no unique privileges. The only common privileges is ALTER.

TABLE

Provides the ability to work with tables. Unique privileges are:

BACKUP ANY
    Gives the privilege to use the Export utility on objects in other users' schemas.

COMMENT ANY
    Gives the privilege to comment on any table, view, or column in any schema.

INSERT ANY
    Gives the privilege to insert rows into tables in other users' schemas.

LOCK ANY
  Gives the privilege to lock tables and views in other users' schemas.

FLASHBACK ANY
  Gives the ability to issue a SQL flashback query on any table, view, or materialized view in other users' schemas. You can still use the DBMS_FLASHBACK built-in package's procedures without this privilege.

UPDATE ANY
  Gives the privilege to update rows in tables and views in other users' schemas.

See also the entry on FLASHBACK ANY TABLE under "Miscellaneous privileges" later in this section.

Common privileges are CREATE [ANY] (CREATE supported only in Oracle8 Database and before), ALTER ANY, DELETE ANY, DROP ANY, and SELECT ANY.

TABLESPACES

Provides the ability to work with tablespaces. Unique privileges are:

MANAGE
  Gives the privilege to take tablespaces offline and online and to begin and end tablespace backups.

UNLIMITED TABLESPACE
  Gives the privilege to override any specific tablespace quotas assigned. If this privilege is revoked, a user cannot allocate an additional tablespace unless allowed by existing tablespace quotas. This privilege cannot be granted to a role.

Common privileges are CREATE, ALTER, and DROP.

TRIGGER

Provides the ability to work with triggers. The only unique privilege is:

ADMINISTER DATABASE
  Gives the privilege to create a trigger on the database. To obtain this privilege, the user or role must also have the CREATE [ANY] TRIGGER privilege.

Common privileges are CREATE [ANY], ALTER ANY, and DROP.

TYPES

Provides the ability to work with user-defined types. The only unique privilege is:

UNDER ANY
> Gives the privilege to create subtypes under any types not defined as final.

Common privileges are CREATE [ANY], ALTER ANY, DROP ANY, and EXECUTE ANY.

USER

Provides the ability to work with database users. The only unique privilege is:

BECOME
> Gives the privilege to become another user, which is required to perform a full database import.

Common privileges are CREATE, ALTER, and DROP.

VIEW

Provides the ability to work with views. The only unique privilege is:

UNDER ANY
> Gives the privilege to create subviews under any object view.

See also the entry for FLASHBACK ANY TABLE under "Miscellaneous Privileges." The common privileges are CREATE [ANY] and DROP.

Miscellaneous privileges

The following system privileges do not fall into any of the earlier categories:

ANALYZE ANY
> Gives the privilege to analyze any table, cluster, or index in any schema.

EXEMPT ANY
> Gives the privilege to bypass application-driven security policies.

FLASHBACK ANY TABLE
> Gives the privilege to issue a SQL flashback query on any table, view, or materialized view in any schema. Note that even without this privilege you can use the DBMS_FLASHBACK built-in package's procedures.

FORCE TRANSACTION
> Gives the privilege to force the commit or rollback of any of the user's distributed transactions in the local database.

FORCE ANY TRANSACTION
> Gives the privilege to force the commit or rollback of any distributed transaction in the local database or induce the failure of a distributed transaction.

GRANT ANY PRIVILEGE
> Gives the privilege to grant any system privilege.

GRANT ANY OBJECT PRIVILEGE
> Gives the privilege to grant any object privilege.

[GLOBAL] QUERY REWRITE
> Gives the privilege to enable query rewrite on a materialized view or to create a function-based index. The GLOBAL keyword acts like the ANY keyword.

RESUMABLE
> Gives the privilege to enable resumable space allocation.

SELECT ANY DICTIONARY
> Gives the privilege to query any data dictionary object in the SYS schema, which lets the user selectively override the setting of the O7_DICTIONARY_ACCESSIBILITY initialization parameter.

Special system privileges

The following system privileges are used to give the user permission to perform an entire set of operations. These system privileges are special because a single privilege grants multiple underlying permissions.

SYSDBA

> Gives a user all the permissions needed to start up and shut down an Oracle database; designed for a DBA. It includes the RESTRICTED SESSION privilege and the following permissions:
>
> > ALTER DATABASE
> > CREATE DATABASE
> > ARCHIVELOG
> > RECOVERY
> > CREATE SPFILE

SYSOPER

> Gives a user a slightly more limited set of permissions; designed for a system operator. It includes the RESTRICTED SESSION privilege and these permissions:
>
> > ALTER DATABASE OPEN | MOUNT | BACKUP
> > ARCHIVELOG
> > RECOVERY
> > CREATE SPFILE

Schema object privileges

The following list describes schema object privileges that can be applied to a number of schema object types.

ALTER

> Changes the definition of the object.

DEBUG

> Accesses PL/SQL code or information about SQL statements that access the object directly through a debugger.

DELETE

> Removes rows from the object.

EXECUTE
    Compiles or executes a procedure or function in the object or accesses a program object declared in the object.

FLASHBACK
    Executes a flashback query on the object.

INSERT
    Adds new rows to the object.

REFERENCES
    Creates a constraint that references the object.

SELECT
    Queries the object.

UNDER
    Creates a subobject at the level below the object.

UPDATE
    Changes existing data in the object.

Each type of schema object is listed in the following sections, along with its unique privileges and any applicable common privileges from the above list.

Directories

Provides privileges to perform operations on directories. Unique privileges are:

READ
    Reads files in a directory.

WRITE
    Writes to files in a directory, with the exception of BFILEs. Applies to external tables in the directory.

There are no common privileges.

External tables

Provides privileges to perform operations on external tables. There are no unique privileges. Common privileges are ALTER and SELECT.

Indextypes

Provides privileges to perform operations on indextype objects. There are no unique privileges. The only common privilege is EXECUTE.

Libraries

Provides privileges to perform operations on libraries. There are no unique privileges. Common privileges are CREATE and DROP.

Materialized views

Provides privileges to perform operations on materialized views. There are no unique privileges. Common privileges are DELETE, FLASHBACK, INSERT, SELECT, UPDATE. The DELETE, INSERT, and UPDATE privileges can be granted only on updatable materialized views.

Operators

Provides privileges to perform operations on user-defined operators. There are no unique privileges. The only common privilege is EXECUTE.

Procedures, functions, and packages

Provides privileges to perform operations on three types of program units: procedures, functions, and packages. There are no unique privileges. Common privileges are DEBUG and EXECUTE.

Sequences

Provides privileges to perform operations on sequences. There are no unique privileges. Common privileges are ALTER and SELECT.

Tables

Provides privileges to perform operations on tables. Unique privileges are:

INDEX
> Creates an index on the table.

ON COMMIT REFRESH
> Creates a materialized view that is refreshed on a COMMIT operation.

QUERY REWRITE
> Creates a materialized view for query rewrite on a specific table.

Common privileges are ALTER, DELETE, DEBUG, FLASH-BACK, INSERT, REFERENCES, SELECT, and UPDATE.

User-defined types

Provides privileges to perform operations on user-defined types. User-defined types are unique datatypes created by a user. There are no unique privileges. Common privileges are DEBUG, EXECUTE, and SELECT.

Views

Provides privileges to perform operations on views. To grant a privilege on a view, you must have that privilege with the GRANT OPTION on all of the view's base tables. There are no unique privileges. Common privileges are DEBUG, DELETE, FLASH-BACK, INSERT, REFERENCES, and SELECT.

Privilege commands

To assign privileges to a user or a role, you use the GRANT command. To remove a privilege from a user or a role, you use the REVOKE command.

The following keywords and clauses are valid for both the GRANT and REVOKE commands:

system_privilege
> A system privilege, as described earlier in the "System privileges" section.

role
> An existing role.

ALL PRIVILEGES

> Grants or revokes all system privileges except SELECT ANY DICTIONARY. For objects, grants all privileges that you have for the object, and the keyword PRIVILEGES is optional.

grantee

> One or more users, roles, or the keyword PUBLIC, which grants or revokes the privilege to all database users. If multiple grantees are specified, they should be separated by commas.

object_privilege

> An object privilege, as described earlier in the "Schema object privileges" section.

column_name

> One or more columns on which to grant or revoke the INSERT, REFERENCES, or UPDATE object privileges. If you do not specify a column, the grantee has privileges on all columns in the table or view.

schema.object

> The object on which to grant or revoke the privilege. If you do not specify a schema, Oracle assumes that the object is in your own schema.

DIRECTORY *directory_name*

> Specifies the directory on which to grant or revoke a privilege.

GRANT

Grants system privileges or roles to a user or role:

```
GRANT {system_privilege | role | ALL PRIVILEGES}
    TO grantee [IDENTIFIED BY password] [WITH ADMIN OPTION]
```

Grants object privileges:

```
GRANT {object_privilege | ALL [PRIVILEGES]}
        [column_name [,column_name ...]]
    ON {schema.object | DIRECTORY directory_name |
        JAVA (SOURCE | RESOURCE) [schema.]object}
    TO grantee [WITH GRANT OPTION] [WITH HIERARCHY OPTION]
```

In order to grant a privilege, you must previously have been granted the privilege or role via WITH ADMIN OPTION, described below. You can also grant privileges if you have GRANT ANY PRIVILEGE (for system privileges), GRANT ANY ROLE (for roles), or GRANT OPTION (for schema objects), or if you own the object. System privileges and schema object privileges cannot be granted in the same GRANT statement.

IDENTIFIED BY *password*
Can be used to identify an existing user by password or to create a new user with the specified password.

ALL PRIVILEGES
Grants all privileges to the user or role, except the SELECT ANY DICTIONARY privilege.

WITH ADMIN OPTION
Allows the user to grant or revoke the system privilege or role or to alter or drop the role.

WITH GRANT OPTION
Like the WITH ADMIN OPTION, allows the user or role to grant or revoke the object privilege to/from other users or roles.

JAVA SOURCE | RESOURCE
Grants access to Java source code or a Java resource.

WITH HIERARCHY OPTION
Allows the grantee to have privilege on all subobjects of the specified schema object.

REVOKE

Revokes system privileges or roles previously granted:

```
REVOKE {system_privilege | role | ALL PRIVILEGES}
    FROM grantee
```

Revokes object privileges:

```
REVOKE {object_privilege | ALL [PRIVILEGES]}
        [column_name [,column_name ...]]
    ON {schema.object | DIRECTORY directory_name |
        JAVA [SOURCE | RESOURCE] [schema.]object}
    FROM grantee [CASCADE CONSTRAINTS] [FORCE]
```

This command can only revoke privileges that were previously granted with the GRANT command. If you revoke a role from a user who currently has it enabled, the role will remain but that user will not be allowed to enable it again.

If multiple grantors have given a privilege to a user (or PUBLIC), all grantors must revoke the privilege before it becomes unavailable to the user.

ALL PRIVILEGES
  Revokes all existing system privileges for the user or role.

JAVA SOURCE | RESOURCE
  Revokes access to Java source code or a Java resource.

CASCADE CONSTRAINTS
  Used only when you revoke the REFERENCES privilege or ALL object privileges. Drops any constraints the revoked user has defined on the object.

FORCE
  Used to revoke the EXECUTE object privilege on objects of user-defined types, when those objects have table or type dependencies. Causes all dependent objects to be marked INVALID, disallows access to data in dependent tables, and marks all dependent function-based indexes as UNUSABLE.

Roles

Granting individual privileges to individual users can incur a substantial amount of overhead, especially for enterprise systems with large numbers of users. Roles are designed to simplify the management of privileges.

Privileges can be granted to roles; users can then be assigned to roles that give them appropriate privileges. Privilege maintenance is performed on roles and affects users with those roles. In addition, roles can be selectively enabled and disabled for users, depending on context. In this way, you can use roles to combine together sets of privileges that will be granted as a whole. For instance, you could have an ADMIN role that would give the appropriate permissions to an administrator.

A role can be granted to another (parent) role. If you give a user the parent role, by default that user will also be granted all of the (child) roles granted to that parent role.

A user can be granted multiple roles. The number of roles that can be enabled at one time is limited by the initialization parameter MAX_ENABLED_ROLES. Multiple roles allow a single user to assume different sets of privileges at different times. If a role has other roles granted to it, using the parent role will have the effect of using all the child roles.

You can set one or more default roles using the ALTER USER statement. Default roles take effect when a user logs in to the Oracle database.

Oracle comes with a number of predefined system roles:

CONNECT
Includes system privileges ALTER SESSION, CREATE CLUSTER, CREATE DATABASE LINK, CREATE SEQUENCE, CREATE SESSION, CREATE SYNONYM, CREATE TABLE, and CREATE VIEW. According to Oracle, this role exists to provide compatibility with earlier releaeses and may not be supported in future releases.

RESOURCE
Includes system privileges CREATE CLUSTER, CREATE INDEXTYPE, CREATE OPERATOR, CREATE PROCEDURE, CREATE SEQUENCE, CREATE TABLE, CREATE INDEX, and CREATE TYPE. According to Oracle, this role exists to provide compatibility with earlier releases and may not be supported in future releases.

DBA
Includes all system privileges with WITH ADMIN OPTION. According to Oracle, this role exists to provide compatibility with earlier releases and may not be supported in future releases.

EXP_FULL_DATABASE

Designed to provide all the privileges necessary to perform full and incremental database exports. Includes system privileges SELECT ANY TABLE, BACKUP ANY TABLE, EXECUTE ANY PROCEDURE, EXECUTE ANY TYPE, ADMINISTER RESOURCE MANAGER, and the INSERT, DELETE, and UPDATE privileges on the SYS. INCVID, SYS.INCFIL, and SYS.INCEXP tables. Also includes the roles EXECUTE_CATALOG_ROLE and SELECT_CATALOG_ROLE.

IMP_FULL_DATABASE

Designed to provide all the privileges necessary to perform full database imports. Includes many system privileges, along with the EXECUTE_CATALOG_ROLE and SELECT_CATALOG_ ROLE roles.

DELETE_CATALOG_ROLE

Includes the DELETE privilege on the system audit table (AUD$).

EXECUTE_CATALOG_ROLE

Includes the EXECUTE privilege on the system audit table (AUD$) and the HS_ADMIN_ROLE role.

SELECT_CATALOG_ROLE

Includes the SELECT privilege on the system audit table (AUD$) and the HS_ADMIN_ROLE role.

RECOVERY_CATALOG_OWNER

Designed to provide all the privileges necessary for the owner of the recovery catalog. Includes system privileges CREATE SESSION, ALTER SESSION, CREATE CLUSTER, CREATE DATABASE LINK, CREATE PROCEDURE, CREATE SEQUENCE, CREATE SYNONYM, CREATE TABLE, CREATE TRIGGER, and CREATE VIEW.

HS_ADMIN_ROLE

Designed to protect Heterogeneous Services (HS) data dictionary views and packages.

AQ_ADMINISTRATOR_ROLE
  Designed to provide privileges necessary to administer
  Advanced Queuing. Includes ENQUEUE ANY QUEUE,
  DEQUEUE ANY QUEUE, MANAGE ANY QUEUE,
  and SELECT privileges on Advanced Queuing tables,
  along with EXECUTE privileges on Advanced Queuing
  packages.

SNMPAGENT
  Used by the Enterprise Manager Intelligent Agent and
  includes the ANALYZE ANY and SELECT privileges on
  various views.

The commands described below allow you to create, alter,
and drop roles.

You can set one or more default roles using the ALTER
USER command. Default roles take effect when a user logs in
to the Oracle database.

CREATE ROLE

Creates a role.

```
CREATE ROLE rolename {NOT IDENTIFIED | IDENTIFIED
    {EXTERNALLY | GLOBALLY | BY PASSWORD |
        USING [schema.]package}}
```

When you create a role, it is automatically granted to you as a
default role.

NOT IDENTIFIED
  Specifies that no password is required for the role.

IDENTIFIED
  Indicates how the user will be authenticated before being
  allowed to enable the role or assume the role as a default role.
  Options are:

  BY PASSWORD
    Local user must provide password to enable role.

  USING [schema.]package
    A package will verify the user. Used for application roles.
    If a schema name is not provided, the package is assumed
    to be in your schema.

EXTERNALLY
> External user is authorized by a third-party service, like the operating system.

GLOBALLY
> User is authorized by an enterprise directory service.

ALTER ROLE

Alters how the user of a role is authenticated.

```
CREATE ROLE rolename {NOT IDENTIFIED | IDENTIFIED
    {EXTERNALLY | GLOBALLY | BY PASSWORD |
        USING [schema.]package}}
```

The keywords are identical to the keywords listed for the CREATE ROLE command.

DROP ROLE

Drops a role from the database.

```
DROP ROLE role_name
```

If a user currently has the role enabled, that user will not be immediately affected but will not be allowed to enable the role again.

SET ROLE

Enables one or more roles for a user or disables all roles for a user.

```
SET ROLE {role [IDENTIFIED BY password]
    [, role [IDENTIFIED BY PASSWORD_ ... ]] |
    ALL [EXCEPT role[, role_ ... ]]
    NONE}
```

ALL
> Enables all roles granted to a user.

EXCEPT
> Used to exclude some roles from being enabled with the ALL keyword.

NONE
> Used to disable all roles for the user.

Auditing

Just as monitoring resource usage is an important way to understand performance issues, auditing is a way to track usage in the database and to become aware of potential security issues.

For some time, Oracle has allowed three different types of auditing:

Statement auditing
Audits the statements issued on the database for specific users or for all users.

Privilege auditing
Audits the use of system privileges for specific users or for all users.

Schema object auditing
Audits a specific set of SQL statements on a particular schema object.

Oracle9*i* Database and Oracle Database 10*g* also allow a fourth type of auditing, called *fine-grained auditing*, which is explained later, in the "Fine-grained auditing" section.

For all types of auditing, Oracle writes audit records to one of these locations: a database audit trail; the SYS.FGA_LOG$ table; or an operating system file (in binary format). The audit trail records contain different information, depending on the type of auditing and the options set for the auditing.

Whether or not auditing is enabled for your Oracle database, the following actions always generate records for the operating system audit trail:

- Instance startup
- Instance shutdown
- Access by users with administrator privileges

You enable and disable auditing with the AUDIT and NOAUDIT commands as described below.

AUDIT

Enables auditing on your Oracle database.

```
AUDIT sql_statement_clause | schema_object_clause
    [BY SESSION | ACCESS]
    [WHENEVER [NOT] SUCCESSFUL]
```

sql_statement_clause
This clause is used to specify statement and system privilege auditing and has the following syntax:

```
{[statement_option | ALL][, ...]} |
    {[system_privilege | ALL PRIVILEGES] [, ...]}
    BY {proxy(, proxy ...,]
        ON BEHALF OF [{user [, user ...] |
            ANY | {user[, user ...]}
```

schema_object_clause
This clause is used to specify schema object auditing and has the following syntax:

```
{object_option[, object_option ...] | ALL }
    ON {[schema.]object | DIRECTORY
            directory_ name | DEFAULT }
```

BY SESSION | ACCESS
Specifies whether you want an audit record written once for each session or each time a particular type of access is attempted. Statement auditing and privilege auditing on DDL statements can be set only BY ACCESS.

WHENEVER [NOT] SUCCESSFUL
WHENEVER SUCCESSFUL specifies that only SQL statements that succeed are audited. With the NOT keyword, the only statements audited are those that fail or result in errors because of insufficient privileges or because a referenced object does not exist. The default if this keyword is not used is to audit all statements, regardless of whether they succeed or fail.

BY *user*
Specifies auditing on the basis of one or more usernames.

BY *proxy* ON BEHALF OF
Specifies auditing of actions taken by a proxy on behalf of a user.

statement_option
The values for this keyword and the statements each value will audit for that type of object are given in the following two lists. The first list shows the statements that are audited if you specify the ALL keyword.

CLUSTER
CREATE, AUDIT, DROP, TRUNCATE

CONTEXT
CREATE, DROP

[PUBLIC] DATABASE LINK
CREATE, DROP

DIMENSION
CREATE, ALTER, DROP

DIRECTORY
CREATE, DROP

INDEX
CREATE, ALTER, DROP

NOT EXISTS
All statements that fail because an object does not exist.

PROCEDURE
CREATE FUNCTION, CREATE LIBRARY, CREATE PACKAGE, CREATE PACKAGE BODY, CREATE PROCEDURE, DROP FUNCTION, DROP LIBRARY, DROP PACKAGE, DROP PROCEDURE

PROFILE
CREATE, ALTER, DROP

ROLE
CREATE, ALTER, DROP, SET

ROLLBACK SEGMENT
CREATE, ALTER, DROP

SEQUENCE
CREATE, DROP

SESSION
Logons for the session.

[PUBLIC] SYNONYM
   CREATE, DROP

SYSTEM AUDIT
   AUDIT system privileges and roles; NOAUDIT system
   privileges and roles

SYSTEM GRANT
   GRANT system privileges and roles; REVOKE system
   privileges and roles

TABLE
   CREATE, DROP, TRUNCATE

TABLESPACE
   CREATE, ALTER, DROP

TRIGGER
   CREATE, ALTER with ENABLE or DISABLE clauses,
   DROP, ALTER TABLE with ENABLE or DISABLE clauses

TYPE
   CREATE, CREATE TYPE BODY, ALTER, DROP, DROP
   TYPE BODY

USER
   CREATE, ALTER, DROP

VIEW
   CREATE, DROP

The second list shows keywords whose statements are
audited if you do not specify the ALL keyword. Unless
otherwise noted, each keyword causes auditing only on
the statement it specifies.

ALTER SEQUENCE

ALTER TABLE

COMMENT TABLE
   Audits COMMENT statements on table, view, materialized view, or columns in each of these objects.

DELETE TABLE

EXECUTE PROCEDURE
   Audits CALL.

GRANT DIRECTORY
   Audits GRANT and REVOKE on directory.

GRANT PROCEDURE
: Audits GRANT and REVOKE on procedure.

GRANT SEQUENCE
: Audits GRANT and REVOKE on sequence.

GRANT TABLE
: Audits GRANT and REVOKE on table, view, or materialized view.

GRANT TYPE
: Audits GRANT and REVOKE on type.

INSERT TABLE
: Audits INSERT INTO table or view.

LOCK TABLE
: Audits LOCK table or view.

SELECT SEQUENCE
: Audits any statement containing CURRVAL or NEXTVAL for the sequence.

SELECT TABLE
: Audits SELECT FROM table, view, or materialized view.

UPDATE TABLE
: Audits UPDATE table or updatable view.

ALL (*statement_option*)
: See the definition of *statement_option* in the previous list for a list of the statements ALL will audit.

system_privilege
: Specifies the system privileges to audit. You can specify the CONNECT, RESOURCE, or DBA role to audit all the system privileges included in that role.

ALL PRIVILEGES
: Audits all system privileges.

proxy
: Specifies whether to audit all actions by a proxy or only those taken by the proxy on behalf of a particular user.

user
: Specifies the user(s) to be audited.

object_option
> Each object has one or more types of access that can be audited. Objects and their auditing options are:

Context
> GRANT

Directory
> AUDIT, GRANT, READ

Library
> GRANT, READ

Materialized view
> ALTER, AUDIT, COMMENT, DELETE, INDEX, INSERT, LOCK, RENAME, SELECT, UPDATE

Object type
> ALTER, AUDIT, GRANT

Procedure, function, package
> AUDIT, EXECUTE, GRANT, RENAME; this type of auditing is available in PL/SQL or Java

Sequence
> ALTER, AUDIT, GRANT, SELECT

Table
> ALTER, AUDIT, COMMENT, DELETE, GRANT, INDEX, INSERT, LOCK, RENAME, SELECT, UPDATE

View
> AUDIT, COMMENT, DELETE, GRANT, INSERT, LOCK, RENAME, SELECT, UPDATE

[schema.]object
> Object to be audited. If the schema is not present, Oracle assumes that the object is in your schema.

directory_name
> Name of the directory to be audited.

DEFAULT
> Sets the default auditing options for all objects created after this statement is issued.

NOAUDIT

```
NOAUDIT sql_statement_clause | schema_object_clause
    [BY SESSION | ACCESS]
```

Turns off any previously started audits. The keywords and clauses for NOAUDIT have the same meaning as for the AUDIT statement.

Other Security Features

The security features described in the following sections are most relevant to Oracle system administrators or security administrators. We provide only a brief overview of these features; see the Oracle documentation for complete details.

Views

In addition to the security features described in previous sections, *views* are commonly used to limit access to data. With a view, you define a subset of data in a table based on the data values and then grant the user access to that view. You can achieve the same "security by selection" with the use of fine-grained access control (see "Fine-grained access control and security policy").

Stored procedures

You can impose a similar limitation by granting users access to a table only through a stored procedure or package. In addition, the stored procedure can have its own validation rules within its code.

Fine-grained access control and security policy

Fine-grained access control (FGAC) provides the type of context-sensitive security that used to be implemented in application code or views. But because FGAC is enforced by the database, it is consistently applied across all applications.

FGAC is implemented by having a security policy associated with a table implement security on that table. The *security policy* is a program unit that can grant access based on any kind of logical condition. The security policy creates a *predicate* (a condition added to the WHERE clause to limit data accessed) for any SQL statements issued against the database; the predicate can be used to implement security based on the content of data in the table.

Virtual Private Database

Content-sensitive security can be used to implement a Virtual Private Database, or VPD. With a VPD, many different users can essentially see their own views of one or more tables in the database. Views are another way of implementing this type of security, but a VPD avoids the overhead of creating views and having different users, or groups of users, access different database views.

Label security and Policy Manager

Label security is an extension of the VPD that is available as an add-on product for Enterprise Edition. It provides program units that act on the value in a single column, which contains the label; implementing it requires no additional programming.

Policy Manager, a GUI management tool that is a part of Enterprise Manager, allows you to implement label security.

Application contexts

Application contexts provide a way to allow certain attributes to be set for a user that last for the duration of the user's session. By using these attributes to grant access, you can create an application-dependent role that persists in the database across different portions of the application. Application contexts can be used to implement FGAC.

Fine-grained auditing

Like FGAC, fine-grained auditing is implemented by defining a predicate to limit the SQL statements that will be audited. By using these audit policies, you can focus auditing activity on a small set of vital data. Reducing the overall number of audit records makes it much easier to spot potential security violations.

LogMiner

LogMiner is a tool that lets you use SQL statements to analyze events in the database log. With LogMiner, you can track transactions as they are processed or locate specific functions that result in data modifications. LogMiner can be used, along with audit trails, to determine what has happened in your Oracle database. A LogMiner viewer is included as part of Enterprise Manager.

Oracle Advanced Security

Oracle Advanced Security (formerly known as Secure Network Services and then as Advanced Network Services) is an add-on package that provides encryption services. Oracle Advanced Security provides additional security functionality in three main areas:

Network security
> Includes support for encrypting messages going over Oracle Net Services; Secure Sockets Layer (SSL) encryption; and RADIUS, Kerberos, smart cards, token cards, and biometric authentication.

Enterprise user security
> Includes support for a wide variety of third-party directory protocols, such as LDAP (Lightweight Directory Access Protocol), which can be used to implement single sign-on capability. OID is included with Oracle Advanced Security. (LDAP and OID are discussed in more detail later, in the "Oracle Internet Directory" section.)

Public key infrastructure security
Includes support for standard X.509 Version 3 certificates. Oracle works with major PKI service vendors, such as Baltimore Technologies and VeriSign, to ensure coordination with their trusted roots.

Oracle Advanced Security embeds these services in the Oracle Net Services layer, which implements communications between a client and a server. Oracle Advanced Security can also be used with a thin Java DataBase Connectivity (JDBC) driver that does not include Oracle Net Services.

Oracle Advanced Security includes Oracle Enterprise Security Manager, a GUI tool for managing enterprise users and domains.

NOTE

If you are not running Oracle Advanced Security, you can still encrypt data on your server through the use of the DBMS_CRYPTO built-in package (or, prior to Oracle Database 10g, DBMS_OBFUSCATION_TOOLKIT).

Oracle Internet Directory

An *external directory* is a way to store information about a database, such as usernames and permissions. An external directory can relate to many different instances of Oracle across an enterprise. Oracle has its own external directory offering, OID, which is a fully compliant LDAP directory. LDAP is a directory access protocol that was developed at the University of Michigan.

With OID or other LDAP directories, you can create an authentication method that can span multiple databases, as well as be used for other purposes in your overall IT architecture. OID supports three types of authentication: anonymous, password-based, and certificate-based.

OID includes its own Replication Manager, for support of multiple directories, and a GUI tool.

Invoker rights

Through PL/SQL you can now create a function, procedure, package, object type, or Java code with an invoker rights clause. This clause causes the object to execute with the rights of the user invoking it, rather than the rights of the object itself.

The Data Dictionary

The Oracle data dictionary is a collection of tables and related views that enable you to see the inner workings and structure of the Oracle database. By querying these tables and views, you can obtain information about every object and every user of the database. All of the Oracle monitoring tools look at the information available in the data dictionary and present it in an easy-to-use format.

Traditionally, the data dictionary has consisted of a series of views owned by the SYS user. These views, known as *static data dictionary views*, present information contained in tables that are updated when Oracle processes a DDL statement. The SYS tables and views, as well as a set of public synonyms for the views, are created by the *catalog.sql* script. In addition, the installation of some Oracle features creates tables and views in the SYSTEM schema. In general, tables and views owned by SYSTEM exist to support functionality provided by PL/SQL stored procedures rather than fundamental Oracle functionality.

There is a second set of views known as the *dynamic performance views* and commonly referred to as the *V$ views*. These V$ views are based on a set of internal memory structures maintained by Oracle as virtual tables (which all begin with an "X$" prefix). Just as the static data dictionary views provide information about the database, the V$ views (and underlying X$ tables) provide information about the active instance.

Static Views

While new views are added with every version of Oracle, the static data dictionary views have existed in their current format since Oracle6. These are views owned by SYS that are built upon tables owned by SYS; they provide the ability to access information about database objects.

Families of views

Most of the static data dictionary is constructed in a matrix fashion. The first way to categorize data dictionary views is by the breadth of information they cover. Most views can be divided into three groups:

USER_
> Views that allow you to see objects you own. Most view names begin with USER_ (e.g., USER_TABLES and USER_INDEXES).

ALL_
> Views that allow you to see objects that you own or that you have been granted privileges to access. Most of these view names begin with ALL_ (e.g., ALL_TABLES and ALL_INDEXES).

DBA_
> Views that allow you to see all objects in the database, regardless of who owns them These views are primarily for use by the DBA and most of them begin with DBA_ (e.g., DBA_TABLES and DBA_INDEXES).

There are also a handful of other views that provide information of general interest about the database.

The ALL_ views have the same structure as the DBA_ views. The USER_ views have the same structure as the DBA_ views except that they do not include the OWNER column. The views that exist in multiple forms are listed below in the form *_viewname. So, for example, when you see *_TABLES, this generally means these three views are actually available:

```
ALL_TABLES
DBA_TABLES
USER_TABLES
```

The second way to categorize data dictionary views is by content. Many of the USER_, ALL_, and DBA_ views are grouped in families, or functional categories, often according to how their view names end (e.g., TABLES, COLUMNS, and so on). Groups of views provide information about particular Oracle topics.

The remainder of this section contains a list of static views organized by topic. For more detailed information, see the *Oracle Data Dictionary Pocket Reference* (O'Reilly) or your Oracle documentation.

Advisor views

Oracle Database 10g provides built-in tools for space and data management called *advisors*. The views listed below provide access to the data collected and maintained by Oracle for use by these advisors. Note that there are no ALL_ views in this group.

*_ADVISOR_ACTIONS	Lists recommendations from advisors.
DBA_ADVISOR_COMMANDS	Lists information about commands from advisors.
DBA_ADVISOR_DEFINITIONS	Provides properties for all advisors.
*_ADVISOR_FINDINGS	Lists findings from all advisors.
*_ADVISOR_JOURNAL	Lists journal entries for advisors.
DBA_ADVISOR_LOG	Lists all advisor tasks.
DBA_ADVISOR_OBJECT_TYPES	Lists object types used by advisors.
*_ADVISOR_OBJECTS	Lists all objects referenced by advisors.
*_ADVISOR_PARAMETERS	Lists parameters and their values for all advisor tasks.
*_ADVISOR_RATIONALE	Lists the rationale behind each advisor recommendation.

*_ADVISOR_RECOMMENDATIONS	Lists all advisor recommendations.
*_ADVISOR_SQLA_REC_SUM	Lists rollup information from the access advisor.
*_ADVISOR_SQLA_WK_MAP	Lists workload references from the access advisor.
*_ADVISOR_SQLA_WK_STMTS	Lists workload statements from the access advisor.
*_ADVISOR_SQLW_JOURNAL	Lists journal entries for workload objects.
*_ADVISOR_SQLW_PARAMETERS	Lists workload parameters and their values.
DBA_ADVISOR_SQLW_STMTS	Lists statements in the workload.
DBA_ADVISOR_SQLW_SUM	Provides an aggregated summary of all workload objects.
DBA_ADVISOR_SQLW_TABLES	Lists the workload statements and the tables they reference.
DBA_ADVISOR_SQLW_TEMPLATES	Provides aggregated information on workload templates.
DBA_ADVISOR_TASKS	Lists all advisor tasks.
DBA_ADVISOR_TEMPLATES	Lists all advisor templates.
DBA_ADVISOR_USAGE	Lists the usage of each advisor.

Change Data Capture views

Oracle9i Database introduced the Change Data Capture feature, primarily for data warehouses. It allows a user to create a set of change tables that can be used to publish changes to a set of underlying tables. Its associated views are:

*_SUBSCRIPTIONS	Lists all subscriptions.
*_SUBSCRIBED_TABLES	Lists all published tables that have been subscribed to.
*_SUBSCRIBED_COLUMNS	Lists the columns of published tables that have been subscribed to.
*_SOURCE_TABLES	Lists the links between change tables and their source tables.
*_SOURCE_TAB_COLUMNS	Lists the columns in the source tables that are contained in change tables.

Constraint views

The following views provide information about constraints and the columns included in the constraints:

*_CONS_COLUMNS	Shows which columns are affected by each constraint.
*_CONSTRAINTS	Lists all constraints defined in the database.

Data dictionary views

The following views provide information about the objects in the Oracle data dictionary:

*_CATALOG	Lists all tables, views, sequences, and synonyms in the database.
*_DEPENDENCIES	Lists dependencies between database objects. Used to determine which objects become invalid after other objects are altered or dropped.
DICT_COLUMNS	Lists all columns defined in the data dictionary views.
DICTIONARY	Lists all data dictionary views.
*_OBJECTS	Lists all objects in the database. Note that this name predates the Oracle Objects Option and is not restricted to objects created using the Objects Option.

Index views

The following views provide information about indexes and indexed columns:

*_INDEXES	Lists all indexes.
*_IND_COLUMNS	Lists all indexed columns.
DBA_IND_EXPRESSIONS	Lists all indexed expressions.
*_JOIN_IND_COLUMNS	Describes the columns used in the join that the bitmapped index is associated with.
INDEX_HISTOGRAM	Contains information about the distribution of index keys within the table. Populated for one index at a time by the ANALYZE INDEX ... VALIDATE STRUCTURE command.
INDEX_STATS	Contains information about the structure of an index. Populated for one index at a time by the ANALYZE INDEX ... VALIDATE STRUCTURE command.

Jobs and Advanced Queuing views

The following views provide information about the job queues managed by the Oracle built-in package DBMS_JOBS. These job queues are used by the replication facilities and by Oracle Enterprise Manager, but are available for use by any application. Views providing information about the AQ message queues are also included here:

*_ATTRIBUTE_TRANSFORMATIONS	Lists all of the transformation functions for these transformations. Note that there is no ALL_ATTRIBUTE_TRANSFORMATIONS view.
*_JOBS	Lists all jobs defined.
*_JOBS_RUNNING	Lists all currently running jobs.
*_QUEUE_SCHEDULES	Shows when particular queued messages are to be delivered.
*_QUEUE_TABLES	Lists the tables used to hold the queues defined as part of the Oracle Advanced Queuing (AQ) facility.
*_QUEUES	Lists the queues defined as part of the AQ facility.
DBA_TRANSFORMATIONS	Provides information about AQ message transformations.

Lock views

The following views provide information about the current status of locks in the database:

*_BLOCKERS	Lists all sessions holding locks for whose release others are waiting.
*_DDL_LOCKS	Lists all existing DDL (Data Definition Language) locks.
*_DML_LOCKS	Lists all existing DML (Data Manipulation Language) locks.
*_KGL_LOCKS	Lists all KGL (Kernel Generic Library) cache locks in the database
*_LOCK_INTERNAL	Contains internal information for each lock defined in *_LOCKS.

*_LOCKS	Lists all locks held or requested in the database.
*_WAITERS	Lists all sessions that are waiting on a lock held by another session.
DBMS_LOCK_ALLOCATED	Shows which locks the current user has allocated.

Log group views

A *log group* is used to multiplex standby log files across different locations, for the purpose of reducing the impact of a disk failure disaster on the recovery process. The following views provide information about log groups:

| *_LOG_GROUPS | Lists the tables that are associated with log groups. |
| *_LOG_GROUP_COLUMNS | Lists the columns assigned to log groups. |

Materialized view views

A *materialized view* is a view that is used to speed up data warehouse queries with precalculated aggregates. The following views provide information about materialized views:

| *_BASE_TABLE_MVIEWS | Lists information about existing materialized views. |
| *_MVIEW_LOGS | Lists information about materialized view logs, which track changes to the master tables that can be used to refresh the materialized views. |

Networking and distributed transaction views

The following views provide information about the status of Oracle networking, remote databases, and distributed transactions to these remote databases:

*_2PC_NEIGHBORS	Contains information about the commit point for distributed transactions listed in *_2PC_PENDING.
*_2PC_PENDING	Lists information about distributed transactions requiring recovery.
*_DB_LINKS	Lists all database links.

*_PENDING_TRANSACTIONS	Contains further information used by XA for distributed transactions listed in *_2PC_PENDING.
GLOBAL_NAME	Shows the value of the global name. Can be used to determine which database the application is connected to.
TRUSTED_SERVERS	Specifies which servers have been identified as trusted.

Objects Option views

The following views provide information relating to objects created using Oracle's Objects Option, including LOBs:

*_COLL_TYPES	Lists collection types created.
*_DIRECTORIES	Lists all defined external directories where BFILEs are stored.
*_LOBS	Lists all Large Objects defined in the database.
*_METHOD_PARAMS	Lists all parameters for methods defined in *_TYPE_METHODS.
*_METHOD_RESULTS	Lists all method results for methods defined in *_TYPE_METHODS.
*_NESTED_TABLES	Lists all nested tables created using features from the Objects Option.
*_OBJECT_TABLES	Lists all tables created using features from the Objects Option.
*_REFS	Lists the REF columns and attributes for objects.
*_TYPE_METHODS	Lists methods created to support each type defined in *_TYPES.
*_TYPES	Lists all types created.

Partitioning views

The following views provide information about partitioned tables and indexes:

*_IND_PARTITIONS	Lists all index partitions. There is one row for each index partition.
*_IND_SUBPARTITIONS	Lists all index subpartitions. There is one row for each index subpartition.

*_PART_COL_STATISTICS	Contains distribution information about partitioned columns that have been analyzed—for example, *_TAB_COL_STATISTICS for partitioned tables.
*_PART_HISTOGRAMS	Contains information about histograms created on individual partitions.
*_PART_INDEXES	Lists all partitioned indexes. There is one row for each partitioned index.
*_PART_KEY_COLUMNS	Lists the partition key columns for all partitions.
*_PART_TABLES	Lists all partitioned tables. There is one row for each partitioned table.
*_TAB_PARTITIONS	Lists all table partitions. There is one row for each table partition.
*_TAB_SUBPARTITIONS	Lists all table subpartitions. There is one row for each table subpartition.

Programming and PL/SQL views

The following views provide information about PL/SQL stored programs, including functions, procedures, packages, and triggers:

*_ARGUMENTS	Lists all valid arguments for stored procedures and functions. Note that there is no DBA_ARGUMENTS view.
*_ERRORS	Shows all errors from compiling objects.
*_LIBRARIES	Lists the external libraries that can be called from PL/SQL packages, procedures, and functions.
*_OBJECT_SIZE	Shows the size of the compiled code for each PL/SQL package, procedure, function, and trigger.
*_PROCEDURES	Lists information about procedures defined within the database, such as whether they are aggregate functions, pipelined table functions, or parallel-enabled functions..
*_SOURCE	Shows PL/SQL source for packages, procedures, and functions.
*_STORED_SETTINGS	Provides information about persistent parameter settings for stored PL/SQL units.
*_TRIGGER_COLS	Lists columns that are referenced in triggers.
*_TRIGGERS	Shows PL/SQL code for database triggers.
PUBLIC_DEPENDENCY	Lists dependencies using only object numbers.

Replication views

The following views provide information used by Oracle's advanced replication facilities. Oracle currently recommends using the Replication Manager to obtain the information in these views:

*_REGISTERED_MVIEWS	Lists registered materialized views.
*_REGISTERED_MVIEW_GROUPS	Lists registered materialized view groups.
*_REGISTERED_SNAPSHOTS	Lists registered snapshots.
*_REGISTERED_SNAPSHOT_GROUPS	Lists registered snapshot groups.
*_REPAUDIT_ATTRIBUTE	Lists replication audit attributes.
*_REPAUDIT_COLUMN	Lists replication audit columns.
*_REPCAT	Lists the interim status of any asynchronous administrative requests and any error messages generated.
*_REPCATLOG	Lists the interim status of any asynchronous administrative requests and any error messages generated.
*_REPCOLUMN	Lists replicated columns for a group.
*_REPCOLUMN_GROUP	Lists column groups defined for a table. Note that there is no USER_REPCOLUMN_GROUP.
*_REPCONFLICT	Lists tables with replication conflict resolution methods and the methods for the tables. Note that there is no USER_REPCONFLICT view.
*_REPDDL	Lists DDL for replication objects.
*_REPGENOBJECTS	Lists objects generated to support replication.
*_REPGROUP	Lists users who are registered for object group privileges.
*_REPGROUPED_COLUMN	Lists columns in column groups for each table.
*_REPKEY_COLUMNS	Lists information about primary key columns for replicated tables.

*_REPOBJECT	Lists objects in each replicated object group.
*_REPPARAMETER_COLUMN	Lists information about columns used to resolve conflicts.
*_REPPRIORITY	Lists value and priority level of each priority group.
*_REPPRIORITY_GROUP	Lists priority and site priority groups for a replicated object group.
*_REPPROP	Lists technique used to propagate an object.
*_REPRESOL_STATS_CONTROL	Lists information for statistics collection for conflict resolution.
*_REPRESOLUTION	Lists routines used to resolve conflicts for a given schema.
*_REPRESOLUTION_METHOD	Lists conflict resolution routines.
*_REPRESOLUTION_STATISTICS	Lists information about resolved replication conflicts.
*_REPSITES	Lists members of replicated objects group.
DEFCALLDEST	Lists destinations for each deferred remote procedure call.
DBA_REPEXTENSIONS	Lists current operations that are adding new master sites to a master group without quiescing the master group.
DBA_REPSITES_NEW	Lists the new replication sites that you plan to add to your replication environment.

Scheduler views

The following views provide information about Oracle's scheduler. These views were introduced in Oracle Database 10g.

*_SCHEDULER_JOB_ARGS	Lists arguments for all scheduler jobs.
*_SCHEDULER_JOB_CLASSES	Lists classes of all scheduler jobs. Note that there is no USER_ view.
*_SCHEDULER_JOB_LOG	Provides a log of all scheduler jobs.

`*_SCHEDULER_JOB_RUN_DETAILS`	Provides run details for all scheduler jobs.
`*_SCHEDULER_JOBS`	Lists all scheduler jobs.
`*_SCHEDULER_PROGRAM_ARGS`	Lists arguments for all scheduler programs.
`*_SCHEDULER_PROGRAMS`	Lists all scheduler programs.
`*_SCHEDULER_RUNNING_JOBS`	Lists all running scheduler jobs.
`*_SCHEDULER_SCHEDULES`	Lists all schedules for the scheduler.
`*_SCHEDULER_WINDOW_DETAILS`	Lists details for all scheduler windows. Note that there is no USER_ view.
`*_SCHEDULER_WINDOW_GROUPS`	Lists all scheduler window groups. Note that there is no USER_ view.
`*_SCHEDULER_WINDOW_LOG`	Provides log information for all scheduler windows. Note that there is no USER_ view.
`*_SCHEDULER_WINDOWS`	Lists all scheduler windows. Note that there is no USER_ view.
`*_SCHEDULER_WINGROUP_MEMBERS`	Lists the members of all scheduler window groups. Note that there is no USER_ view.

Security and auditing views

The following views provide information about users, grants, and security policies that implement FGAC, as well as information about the status of Oracle auding and audit trails:

`ALL_DEF_AUDIT_OPTS`	Lists the default auditing options in effect for new objects.
`*_APPLICATION_ROLES`	Describes all application roles that have authentication policy roles defined for them. Note that there is no ALL_ view.
`AUDIT_ACTIONS`	Lists the audit codes and descriptions.
`DBA_AUDIT_EXISTS`	Contains audit trail information generated by AUDIT EXISTS and AUDIT NOT EXISTS.
`DBA_AUDIT_OBJECT`	Contains audit trail information for object auditing.
`*_AUDIT_POLICY_COLUMNS`	Lists all fine-grained audit columns. New with Oracle Database 10g.
`DBA_AUDIT_SESSION`	Contains audit trail information for all connects and disconnects.

DBA_AUDIT_STATEMENT	Contains audit trail information for all audited statements.
DBA_AUDIT_TRAIL	Contains all audit trail information.
*_COL_PRIVS	Lists all column grants made in the database.
DBA_COMMON_AUDIT_TRAIL	Lists all standard and fine-grained audit trail entries. New with Oracle Database 10g.
*_GLOBAL_CONTEXT	Lists all the global contexts (sets of application-defined attributes that can be used to determine access rights available to the instance). Note that there is no USER_GLOBAL_CONTEXT view.
*_OBJ_AUDIT_OPTS	Lists all object auditing options in effect. Note that there is no ALL_OBJ_AUDIT_OPTS view.
*_POLICY_CONTEXTS	Lists policies and their associated contexts.
*_POLICY_GROUPS	Lists the various groups for the different security policies.
*_PRIV_AUDIT_OPTS	Lists all system privilege auditing options in effect.
*_PROFILES	Lists all defined profiles.
RESOURCE_COST	Shows the assigned cost of each resource for composite limits.
RESOURCE_MAP	Maps profile resource numbers to resource names.
*_ROLE_PRIVS	Lists all roles granted to users and to other roles.
ROLE_ROLE_PRIVS	Lists roles granted to other roles. A subset of *_ROLE_PRIVS.
ROLE_SYS_PRIVS	Lists only system privileges granted to roles.
ROLE_TAB_PRIVS	Lists table grants granted to roles.
*_ROLES	Lists all roles.
SESSION_PRIVS	Shows which system privileges are active for the current session.
SESSION_ROLES	Shows which roles are active for the current session.
*_STMT_AUDIT_OPTS	Lists all statement auditing options in effect.
STMT_AUDIT_OPTION_MAP	Lists the valid SQL statements that can be specified for statement auditing.
*_SYS_PRIVS	Shows which system privileges have been assigned to which users.

SYSTEM_PRIVILEGE_MAP	Lists the valid system privileges that can be specified for system privilege auditing.
*_TAB_PRIVS	Shows all object privileges.
TABLE_PRIVILEGE_MAP	Lists the valid object audit options that can be specified for schema object auditing.
USER_PASSWORD_LIMITS	Shows the password limits in effect for the current session.
*_USERS	Lists all users and their basic database-related characteristics. Note that ALL_USERS is an abbreviated view, and that there is no USER_USERS view.

Server information views

The following views provide information about a variety of database parameters and other server information:

DBA_ALERT_HISTORY	Provides a history of all alerts. New in Oracle Database 10g.
*_APPLY_ENQUEUE	Provides access to the SQL Apply enqueue. Note that there is no USER_ view. New in Oracle Database 10g.
*_APPLY_EXECUTE	Lists the SQL Apply execute actions. Note that there is no USER_ view. New in Oracle Database 10g.
*_APPLY_INSTANTIATED_GLOBAL	Provides information about databases with an instantiation SCN. Note that there is no USER_ view. New in Oracle Database 10g.
*_APPLY_INSTANTIATED_SCHEMAS	Provides information about schemas with an instantiation SCN. Note that there is no USER_ view. New in Oracle Database 10g.
NLS_DATABASE_PARAMETERS	Shows the National Language Support (NLS) parameters in effect at the database level.

NLS_INSTANCE_PARAMETERS	Shows the NLS parameters in effect at the instance level.
NLS_SESSION_PARAMETERS	Shows the NLS parameters in effect at the session level.
PRODUCT_COMPONENT_VERSION	Shows the current release level of all installed Oracle options.
SM$VERSION	Shows the Oracle version level packaged for Server Manager to use.
*_PROXIES	Lists information about all proxy connections in the system. Note that there is no ALL_PROXIES view.
*_RESUMABLE	Lists all RESUMABLE statements. When the database runs out of space, these statements allows the DBA to suspend an operation, add more space, and then resume the operation. Note that there is no ALL_RESUMABLE view.
*_SEQUENCES	Lists all sequences in the database.
*_SYNONYMS	Lists all synonyms in the database.
DBA_UNDO_EXTENTS	Lists the commit time of each extent in the UNDO tablespace.

SQLJ views

SQLJ is used to embed static SQL statements into a Java program. The following views provide information about SQLJ objects (composite data structures related to the SQLJ statements that are stored in the Oracle database):

*_SQLJ_TYPES	Describes the SQLJ object types.
*_SQLJ_TYPE_ATTRS	Lists the attributes associated with each SQLJ object type.
*_SQLJ_TYPE_METHODS	Describes the methods associated with each SQLJ object type.

Storage views

The following views provide information about internal storage in the database, including datafiles, tablespaces, free extents, used extents, and segments:

DBA_DATA_FILES	Lists all datafiles comprising the database.
*_EXTENTS	Lists every allocated extent for every segment.
DBA_FREE_SPACE	Lists every free extent. This view, combined with *_EXTENTS, should account for all storage in *_DATA_FILES.
*_FREE_SPACE_COALESCED	Lists every extent that is at the start of a block of free extents.
DBA_ROLLBACK_SEGS	Lists all rollback segments.
*_SEGMENTS	Lists all segments.
*_TABLESPACES	Lists all tablespaces in the database.
*_TS_QUOTAS	Shows the granted quota and used storage in tablespaces by user.

Streams views

Oracle Streams provides for smooth flow and sharing of data and events within a database or between multiple databases. There are no USER_ views in this group. All of the following views are new in Oracle Database 10*g*:

DBA_STREAMS_ADMINISTRATOR	Lists users who are Streams administrators.
*_STREAMS_MESSAGE_CONSUMERS	Lists information about Streams message clients.
*_STREAMS_MESSAGE_RULES	Lists messaging rules for Streams.
*_STREAMS_NEWLY_SUPPORTED	Lists information about tables that are newly supported by Streams.
*_STREAMS_RULES	Lists Streams rules.
*_STREAMS_TRANSFORM_FUNCTION	Lists rule-based transformation functions used by Streams.
*_STREAMS_UNSUPPORTED	Lists tables that are unsupported by Streams.

Table, column, and view views

Tables are the most important building blocks of an Oracle database. These views provide information about tables, columns, clusters, and views:

*_ALL_TABLES	Lists all object and relational tables.
*_CLU_COLUMNS	Lists all cluster keys.
*_CLUSTER_HASH_EXPRESSIONS	Lists the hash values used for the optional cluster hash indexes.
*_CLUSTERS	Lists all clusters in the database.
*_COL_COMMENTS	Shows comments on all table and view columns.
*_EXTERNAL_LOCATIONS	Lists the sources for the external tables.
*_EXTERNAL_TABLES	Describes the attributes of external tables.
*_TAB_COL_STATISTICS	Contains column information about analyzed columns.
*_TAB_COLUMNS	Shows all table and view columns.
*_TAB_COMMENTS	Shows all comments on tables and views.
*_TAB_HISTOGRAMS	Shows all table histograms.
*_TABLES	Shows all relational tables.
*_UPDATABLE_COLUMNS	Lists columns that can be updated in views with joins.

Dynamic Views

The dynamic performance data dictionary views (the V$ views) mainly provide information about the Oracle instance, as well as information that the instance maintains about the database. The views in this category are considered dynamic because their contents change based upon how the instance is performing. The contents of these views are representative of the total instance or cluster workload, rather than the performance of one specific SQL statement.

Availability of dynamic views

Specific dynamic performance views are available based on the status of the instance, as follows:

- Those views that provide information specifically about the instance (e.g., V$PARAMETER) are available as soon as the instance is started.

- Those views that provide information stored in the control files are available once the database has been mounted.

- Those views that provide information about how the kernel is processing SQL statements are available once the database has been opened.

How dynamic views are built

Unlike the static data dictionary views, which are views on existing tables, the dynamic performance views are views on a set of tables that do not physically exist in the database; instead they are actually views on X$ tables, which in turn are representations of internal memory structures in the Oracle instance. For example:

SYS.V_$DATABASE
> A regular view on the *fixed view* V$DATABASE. A fixed view is one that cannot be altered or removed by the database administrator.

V$DATABASE
> A fixed view on GV$DATABASE, with filters to show information only for the current instance.

GV$DATABSE
> A public synonym for the view SYS.GV_$DATABASE.

SYS.GV_$DATABASE
> A view on the fixed view GV$DATABASE.

GV$DATABASE
> A fixed view on the virtual table (a memory structure) X$KCCDI.

Understanding how these views are built is important to understanding how they work. Defined within the Oracle kernel, these hardcoded V$ views are accessible once the instance has been started or once the database has been mounted (depending on the type of information, as explained earlier under "Availability of dynamic views"). Once the database is opened, the normal SQL processing takes over, and the public synonyms referencing the views are used. With public synonyms, the same name is available whether you are connected before the database is opened, or are connected as a user with DBA privileges after the database is opened.

The relatively few V$ views that are only available once the database is open turn out to be true views, based upon X$ or other V$ tables.

Global dynamic performance data dictionary views

The dynamic performance data dictionary views are augmented with a complementary set of global dynamic performance data dictionary views (GV$ views). The V$ views provide information about the instance to which you are connected and its management of the database. The GV$ views provide the same information for all other instances that have the same database mounted; they are primarily of interest in a Real Applications Cluster or Oracle Parallel Server environment.

The global dynamic performance data dictionary views add the column INST_ID to their names, which allows you to identify the instance for which information is being provided.

Index

We'd like to hear your suggestions for improving our indexes. Send email to
index@oreilly.com.

Keep in touch with O'Reilly

wnload examples from our books

.o find example files for a book, go to:
www.oreilly.com/catalog

select the book, and follow the "Examples" link.

2. Register your O'Reilly books

Register your book at *register.oreilly.com*

Why register your books? Once you've registered your O'Reilly books you can:

- Win O'Reilly books, T-shirts or discount coupons in our monthly drawing.
- Get special offers available only to registered O'Reilly customers.
- Get catalogs announcing new books (US and UK only).
- Get email notification of new editions of the O'Reilly books you own.

3. Join our email lists

Sign up to get topic-specific email announcements of new books and conferences, special offers, and O'Reilly Network technology newsletters at:
elists.oreilly.com

It's easy to customize your free elists subscription so you'll get exactly the O'Reilly news you want.

4. Get the latest news, tips, and tools
www.oreilly.com

- "Top 100 Sites on the Web"—PC Magazine
- CIO Magazine's Web Business 50 Awards

Our web site contains a library of comprehensive product information (including book excerpts and tables of contents), downloadable software, background articles, interviews with technology leaders, links to relevant sites, book cover art, and more.

5. Work for O'Reilly

Check out our web site for current employment opportunities:
jobs.oreilly.com

6. Contact us

O'Reilly & Associates
1005 Gravenstein Hwy North
Sebastopol, CA 95472 USA

TEL: 707-827-70 00 or 800-998-9938
(6am to 5pm PST)

FAX: 707-829-0104

order@oreilly.com
> For answers to problems regarding your order or our products.
> To place a book order online, visit:
> *www.oreilly.com/order_new*

catalog@oreilly.com
> To request a copy of our latest catalog.

booktech@oreilly.com
> For book content technical questions or corrections.

corporate@oreilly.com
> For educational, library, government, and corporate sales.

proposals@oreilly.com
> To submit new book proposals to our editors and product managers.

international@oreilly.com
> For information about our international distributors or translation queries. For a list of our distributors outside of North America check out:
> *international.oreilly.com/distributors.html*

adoption@oreilly.com
> For information about academic use of O'Reilly books, visit:
> *academic.oreilly.com*

O'REILLY®

Our books are available at most retail and online bookstores.
To order direct: 1-800-998-9938 • *order@oreilly.com* • *www.oreilly.com*
Online editions of most O'Reilly titles are available at *safari.oreilly.com*